Kiss the Mirror

A Love Letter To Your Best Self

JAMIA JACKSON

NOTE FROM THE AUTHOR

 Hey gorgeous!! My name is Jamia Jackson, but most know me as Mimi. My heart's mission is to inspire women around the world to see their reflection as a symbol of strength, beauty, and divinity.

As a successful entrepreneur, identity transformation coach, and women's empowerment advocate, I am dedicated to helping women overcome imposter syndrome, strengthen their self-concept, and walk boldly in their God-given greatness.

My personal journey is a true testament to what the power of self-love and God can do. I know firsthand what it's like to be sucked in and broken down by the world. I know how it feels to hit rock bottom and feel like there's no point of return. I've experienced the side of life where chaos thrives, creating an environment for self-doubt that leaves you questioning your purpose. But I also know what it's like to walk through that fire and come out stronger, bolder, and unshakable in your purpose.

If you take nothing else from this book, I want you to remember this: You are already enough, you are already worthy, and your greatness is not optional-it's inevitable!

Table of Contents

∞

Your Reflection

∞

I used to have this love-hate relationship with my mirror. Some days, it was my best friend, and other days, my fiercest critic. I'd stand there trying to find that perfect angle where the light hit just right, depending on the mirror to tell me something nice about myself. But no matter what, I could never really see what others saw. I would silently critique myself, "If only I had a cute little forehead, or if only my breasts were bigger." Pregnancy and being in labor twice certainly didn't help.

Be honest: how many times have you stood in the mirror silently assaulting yourself with harsh words? How many times have you been able to look at yourself and feel confident in the reflection you see staring back at you? How often have you been able to take a look at your life and say this is the life I chose?

We've all been there—standing in front of that glass, hoping it'll lie to us, depending on it to tell us something we, ourselves, don't feel or see. Believe it or not, how you perceive yourself has a lot to do with how you live your life and the reflection "you see." Perception interferes with our decision-making, affecting the environments we choose to be present in, our relationships, and the things we believe we are capable of.

In my pursuit of happiness, I've found that the way I perceive myself has been one of my biggest pitfalls, but it has also become my greatest victory. After all, If I felt I deserved "just enough" or my options in life were scarce, I would make scarcity-based decisions. Once I decided to see myself as smart, bold, beautiful, and capable, that's exactly who I became. The fact is, the problem isn't the mirror. The problem is what you choose to see, your perception. Your perception can be your worst enemy or your secret weapon to feeling more fulfilled and abundant. Obviously, this isn't just about the mirror; it's about you. The mirror is merely a reflection of YOUR preferences, YOUR beliefs, and ultimately, YOUR LIFE. I've created a whole new identity for myself. The root: I simply changed the way I saw things. I stopped allowing limiting beliefs and fear of things that didn't exist to stop me from achieving any and everything I'd ever dreamed of.

Take a moment to reflect on the successful women you admire or "look up to." The ones who make you silently think, "this is the woman I yearn to become" or "this is the life I yearn to have." Think about how many times those women are confident, bold, and unapologetic. Almost always! Now, visualize you being that woman. Embodying that version of yourself is what "Kiss The Mirror" is all about. You must develop this energy about you that screams fearless. The only thing that holds you back from becoming this version of yourself is your mindset. You must learn how to escape the programming and the constant need to feel validated or liked. You must escape the idea that if you're confident, you're "too much," "extra," or "full of yourself." You must escape the trap of lies that holds most women back from reaching their full potential, becoming their best self, and living their best life.

"Kiss the Mirror" is not about perfection, its about perception. It's all about getting REAL with yourself, flaws, quirks, and all, embodying an unapologetic form of self-confidence and developing an insane amount of self-worth. No matter what. This read is all about the journey to becoming the best, most aware, most confident version of yourself. It's your backstage pass to discovering the version of you that has been hiding in plain sight. The greatest love story ever told is the one between you and YOU.

Together, you and I will uncover the powerful woman who's been hiding behind layers of self-doubt and limiting beliefs. But, I come bearing gifts, too. The end of each chapter holds a personalized love letter to affirm and ground you into your new identity. Your only requirement is to read these letters to yourself daily in the mirror. These powerful love letters will trigger your subconscious mind and cultivate an easy transition into your new identity. Ultimately, leading you into your new life. So, If you're ready to turn your reflection into your biggest fan and start each day with a wink, a kiss, and a lot of self-love, then grab your favorite lipstick, put on your metaphorical crown, and we will begin. Shall we?

CHAPTER 1

Reflection in the Glass

Meeting the Real You

∞

Let me just say that becoming self-aware is such an underestimated superpower. Transparency and authenticity are so important in this new age. Self-awareness involves being unapologetic about facing one's true self, flaws and all. Becoming more self-aware means recognizing and understanding your own emotions, thoughts, and behavior deeply—way deeper than surface level. Your mission is to become committed to doing the "inside job," understanding each and every part of yourself and how they influence your actions and even your interactions with others.

I used to wonder why each of my romantic relationships felt exactly like the last one. "Why do I keep attracting toxic relationships?" I would ask myself. I was literally getting the same guy in each person I dated. I would constantly find myself "crashing out." At one point, I spent four days in jail. Yes, actual jail. My life was constantly spiraling out of control while I was trying to prove my undying love to somebody's unhinged son. Or daughter. Yes, I was once in a romantic relationship with a female. No surprise, she had an identical set of personality traits to my previous partners—narcissistic, toxic, and nonchalant.

One day, the epiphany came. This girl had been a perfect friend, but the romantic relationship mimicked every relationship I'd had with my exes. From the chaotic rage sessions to the prevalent trust issues, I was finally forced to take a look instead at myself. I had to do the "inside job."

The real, more significant eye-opener was the untimely death of my child's father, Lamont. He was violently murdered in his vehicle in Chester, Pennsylvania, with our 5-year-old son at his side. It devastated my heart but fixed my vision for sure. I really do feel like this was my saving grace, no matter how crazy that might sound. Initially, after his death, my life continued to be the same chaotic mess. In actuality, it wasn't the same chaotic mess; it became a lot worse. I had given up on myself completely. I hit rock bottom. You see, Lamont and I always had a great relationship, even when we were no longer intimately involved. He was always my biggest fan, no matter what. In a sense, I felt like I lived for his approval, or I looked to it to confirm whether or not I was on the 'right' path. When I lost him, I lost my passion, I lost my drive, I lost my confidence, and I lost sight of my purpose.

I will never forget that day, I was without a phone because of the chaos in my toxic relationship. My phone had been crushed into pieces, and I was momentarily sharing a phone with my girlfriend. At this time, I'd consider us drifters. Often living in motels, and our car even. She'd convinced me to quit my job that wasn't paying well and I instead became a street hustler. We rode around and made money in any way we knew how. Stealing, lying, scamming, we found ways. On this particular day, July 24, 2018, we were on our way to orientation for these walk-in jobs we'd heard about at a recycling factory. As we pulled in, her phone rang.

"What's good?" she blurted as she picked up the phone. I heard chattering for a moment. A minute later, she frantically handed me the phone. I initially didn't really view her facial expression as a look of concern because people would always call her looking for me. Plus, we were usually high out of our minds with no care in the world, so how would I have paid attention to that anyway? We'd pump ecstasy and liquor into our bodies as if it were medicine from the moment we opened our eyes.

"Hello," I answered.

"Hi, this is Detective John," the voice replied.

Initially, I became aggravated. A few months before, I'd received the same type of call. That time, it had been from Chester Police. They were calling to let me know that Lamont was being arrested. They stated that my two children were at the scene and needed to be picked up. Poet was my only child at the time. The other child was Lamont's step son. When I arrived at the scene, I saw a disheveled Lamont in the back of the police car. His jacket was ripped, and he appeared to have gone through a struggle. As I approached the car, I saw sadness and defeat in Lamont's eyes. He started to tell me exactly what had happened, but the police quickly rolled the window up and ushered me away. "Just get the kids!" Lamont yelled. That was the last time I saw Lamont alive. He ended up doing about 4 months in jail for driving without a license and was only released because the main officer in charge of the arrest suddenly passed away in his sleep. I always thought that was strange. Lamont was murdered 8 days after his release from jail.

For context, Detective John was probably not the Detective's name, but I honestly can't remember his exact name. The aggravation grew as he continued, "I regret to inform you that there's been an incident with Lamont and your son..."

At first, I thought Lamont had done something stupid again to get himself in trouble, but at the mention of my son, my heart dropped. "Is everything ok?" I asked.

"No, I'm afraid there's been a shooting."

Everything went still. I feel like the world quite literally stopped. "Is my son ok? Is Lamont ok?" I asked frantically.

"We can't release that information over the phone," the detective replied dryly.

"Please, tell me," I begged.

There was a long pause before he eventually replied, "I'm afraid he didn't make it. We need you to pick up your son from the Child Advocacy Center in Media, Pennsylvania."

My entire world changed in that very moment. I began to sob loudly, "No, no, no." My girlfriend quickly grabbed the phone and hung it up. She repeatedly asked me what was wrong.

Eventually, I said, "Lamont is gone. They're saying he's gone." The ride to the Child Advocacy Center was a blur. I sobbed the whole time and was honestly in a state of shock. It just didn't feel real.

When we arrived, the detectives questioned me. They asked for permission to interview Poet as well, but I refused. They stated I would be unable to be part of the interview due to it being an "open investigation," so any information he released would be considered confidential. My son was my best friend, and I knew I had to protect him. What if we knew the person? Was it a trusted individual? How much did Poet actually even see or know? I hadn't even had the opportunity to hear what Poet actually witnessed and remembered yet. Choosing to protect my child and his best interest and safety, I politely declined, and we left.

As we entered the car, everything was silent. "Can we go to the hospital and see my dad?" Poet said, breaking the silence. I began to weep again.

As we arrived at my grandmother's house, we saw friends waiting outside for me to arrive. I didn't have a phone, so I was completely unaware that the incident had even made the news. This was the beginning of the fight for my life and the turning point that changed it forever.

Fast forward, I went to live with my mother, who had been absent for the majority of my life due to a life-long struggle with drug use. She'd recently been released from prison and did some time in a halfway house. I would visit her on her weekend passes, take her to run errands, etc. I had been sleeping in my car and motels for months. All I'd been doing was getting high, getting drunk, and roaming the streets, trying to find ways to make money. When my mother finally graduated from the halfway house program, she asked me to come and stay with her. The main perk was that my girlfriend was able to stay as well. It was like anytime things started to work out for me, she (the girlfriend) would become envious and do things to intentionally throw me off track, mess with my mental health, and lower my confidence. I recognize now that this was a form of spiritual warfare.

We were living in North Philadelphia—an area known for crime, drugs, and excessive murders. I felt like I'd truly hit rock bottom. My life consisted of throwing back ecstasy pills, drinking excessively, and just doing whatever it took to get money in my pockets. I had to reflect on my life and pinpoint all the places I'd gone wrong. One thing I knew for sure was that I couldn't stay there in that sunken place. I had to realize that this was the "me" in the midst of unhealed trauma, not who I was destined to be. I had already started to think of businesses I'd open if I ever got the chance. I constantly wrote business ideas ranging from selling lashes to t-shirts to crafting creative drinks in a notebook. I had a forward vision of being better than where I currently was. I would constantly have visions of myself in that reality. I didn't know how I would make money; I just knew I was determined to figure it out. A few months later, I started a business selling candy drinks and named it "Mimi's Candyland." That was the beginning of entrepreneurship for me. I also landed a job at a local Wendy's—Broad Street, to be exact.

I never did struggle with landing a job. As a kid, I learned the importance of reading, writing, and communicating effectively. Needless to say, I believe this helped me tremendously with communicating and being "likable" and "relatable." I was often hired on the spot and given big responsibilities early on. I quickly became aware of my "gift of gab." I began to see it as an attribute as opposed to seeing it as a flaw. As a child, I'd always been called "obnoxious" or told that I "talked too much" or labeled as "rebellious" for questioning things I didn't understand or agree with. This hindered me from being able to show up for myself significantly, as I feared being perceived as "annoying" or "extra." I decided I would no longer dim my own light or be afraid to speak up for myself. I started to tell people exactly how I felt in the best way I knew how. Yes, I lost friends, a lot of them. I'm actually still losing friends at this stage in my life. But you have to understand that it's all a part of the process. When you become self-aware, you start to realize that a lot of the bonds you've created were trauma bonds or bonds that only thrived from you being a lesser, more watered-down version of yourself. Just because something may give you a temporary feeling of euphoria in the moment does not mean that it's good for you long-term.

I attribute these epiphanies to the quiet time I spent on those long walks from my home on 24th and Cecil B. Moore to Broad Street daily. I had so much time to think, reflect, and be uncomfortably honest with myself. I also attribute these downloads to my spiritual connection with God. Yes, I believe heavily in God and was introduced to the church at a very young age. My dad was previously an ordained pastor, so we practically lived in church for a portion of my life.

During the time I spent in Philly, I had a child to care for and was in one of the worst living situations I'd ever been in my entire life. The house was infiltrated with roaches, the fridge was always empty, and the house was always chaotic. I would often engage in all-out fist fights with my mother and her boyfriend. Publicly! Often times over absolutely nothing at all, other times I was stolen from and wrongly disrespected due to narcissism and straight up jealousy. Again, spiritual warfare. Even at my lowest, others could see my light even when I couldn't. Landing the job at Wendy's made me feel progressive and gave me peace of mind for eight hours and a sense of normalcy. The job was definitely necessary at the moment, but I was also self-aware enough to understand that I had so much more work to do. I knew that if I wanted to get out of my current situation and truly repair my life, I had to take some accountability. I could no longer blame anybody but myself for the position I was in. I'd lost control of my own life. I had no idea anymore who the broken girl I saw in the mirror was.

Eventually, the endless fighting with my mother and her boyfriend made me realize I had to get a place of my own. There was no other option. I kept seeing visions of me living a peaceful life, happy and thriving. However, in my current situation, my belongings were still being stolen, there were constant fist fights, and more and more people were crowding into the small apartment. If things continued this way, my resources would always be exhausted, and I'd never get the opportunity to truly save and build for Poet and I. I realized that this situation was extremely toxic, and no matter how much I grew mentally, being in this particular environment would always make me feel drained and stagnant.

Lucky for me, the pandemic hit. I was forced to quit my job, and my income was replaced with unemployment. I didn't spend a dime. I would save my money, and the money I did spend, I poured into my drink business. The liquor stores in Philadelphia had closed due to the crisis so that meant even more business for me. Eventually, I saved enough to buy another car. Things were finally starting to look up for me. I would still constantly write down the many different things I would sell once I got my place and got settled in. Changing my environment was my main concern.

I met Artist's father shortly after. He would come to North Philly all the time and truly supported me in anything I wanted to do. He even allowed me to drive his spare car until I saved enough to purchase mine. My clunker had died on me rather quickly. Artist's father and his lifestyle reminded me of the other side of life I'd been missing while surrounded by all the trauma, toxicity, and chaos. We would go to restaurants, the beach, the movies. He had a full-time job, a loving family, and his life had a sense of normal that I'd been missing. This fueled my motivation. I was slowly starting to remember times when my life hadn't always been bad. I kept seeing myself in another reality. I craved a better life, and I wanted it bad. The unemployment was ok for the time being, but it simply just wasn't enough—well, for me anyway. I had big ideas.

One day, we arrived home from a 2-day beach trip, and my mom's apartment was eerily quiet. My mom was tucked away in her room with her boyfriend, and my grandmother and her boyfriend were asleep in the back room. My uncle JJ was nowhere to be found. See, my uncle JJ and I were the only ones who'd really made friends in that area. We'd go together to local bars, stores, etc. He was always excited to see me when I returned home from Delaware. Strangely, when I returned, he wasn't home. I went to the back room to ask my grandmother where he was, and she said he'd gone to Delaware the same day I did and hadn't returned yet. I felt a little weird about it, but it wasn't abnormal for him to visit Delaware, so I didn't really think too much about it that night. I was exhausted and genuinely hated being there, so I got Poet ready for bed, and we turned in for the night.

Three days passed, and I had still not heard from Uncle JJ. My gut was telling me that something was wrong. I started asking around to see if anybody had seen or talked to him. At the time, I had a close friend in the area, and he always looked out for me. We can call him Greg. So, I asked Greg if he'd seen my uncle lately, and he replied that he had not. He also said that my uncle hadn't been on what we referred to as the "ave" bumming lucys (loose individual cigarettes). I told Greg to ask around and see if he could get any information. We checked around for him on foot. We visited local bars, asked people he would talk to, and even checked inside an abandoned house. I couldn't ignore my intuition telling me that something wasn't right and that my uncle could possibly be somewhere hurt. Everybody else in the house thought I was overreacting. Greg trusted my instincts because he knew how self-aware and 'deep' I was. Two days later, Greg came banging on my door. As I opened the door, I didn't hide my irritation. "Why are..." I started, but before I could finish, he interrupted me.

"Jamia, something happened to your uncle. You need to contact the police," he said seriously.

I had never seen him this concerned. Well, except for a few days before when I'd chased him in my vehicle and accidentally gone up a one-way, resulting in my car being shot. Yes, actual gunshots with my friend and me in the car. God has always protected me, and I am forever grateful for that. We could have died. There was a bullet hole in my passenger seat just above my friend's head. You can never tell me that God is not real!

Greg began to tell me what'd happened while I was away at the beach. Apparently, there had been a fight between my mom's boyfriend and someone in our neighborhood. Words were exchanged, and it may have gotten physical. This is all alleged because I did not personally witness these particular events. He went on to say the alleged victim in the incident had threatened revenge on our entire house. I instantly became alarmed. My son lives here. Why wouldn't anyone tell me something like this? Especially when I'd been looking for my uncle for days, and no one had mentioned the incident or the threats.

"You need to contact the police," Greg said. My look of confusion must have prompted him to elaborate. "Mimi, I think somebody may have done something to your uncle," Greg continued. I would love to say I was shocked, but it honestly felt as if I'd known all along. I instantly picked up my phone and called the local police to make a missing person's report. They stated that for a missing person's report, they'd have to come out to the scene.

Once they arrived, I told them about how we weren't from the area and how I found it abnormal that my uncle hadn't been home in so many days. They told me that if I wanted to, they'd take me down to the station, contact some local hospitals, jails, etc., and do some footwork to see if they could locate him. When I arrived, I sat with a black male detective. Everybody at the station was very kind to me. The detective picked up the phone and called Temple University Hospital first. He described my uncle to a nurse who stated that they had someone matching his description. She stated the victim was unable to remember much and couldn't really talk a lot. They'd been trying to locate his family. My heart sank. It was my uncle, and he'd been shot and found on a local street as the ambulance rode through the area. He'd been in the hospital for four days. I found him. I'd found my uncle.

Keep in mind this was during the pandemic, and you could not visit people in the hospital. That may have applied to everyone else but not me. I moved just like God sent me because he did. When I arrived, I told them he'd been reported missing and demanded to see him, even if only for a minute. If I didn't physically lay eyes on him, to me, he was still a missing person. They announced that somebody had come to see him, and he instantly uttered, "My niece." It indeed was me. They allowed me to lay eyes on him for just a minute and then escorted me out.

When I arrived back home, my mom, her boyfriend, her mother, and even the dog had fled. Poet and I gathered all of our belongings and stayed with Artist's dad for the time being. This was the beginning of me realizing exactly who I was.

This testimony was added not only to show you that God is real and His love is amazing but also to show you just a snippet of the chaos my life has been full of. I hope this helped you understand a little more about my background and the work it took to rebuild myself and reconnect with my power and divinity. This is only a small portion of the trauma I've been through, but it is still very significant. This was my breakthrough and the beginning of my transformation. It all started with me becoming in tune with my body, my higher consciousness, and my self-awareness.

When becoming self-aware, you must be willing to reflect on your experiences, understand how your emotions have affected your decision-making, and recognize the impact this has had on your life. Self-awareness is a foundational element of personal growth and emotional intelligence. It involves deeply understanding your personality, strengths, weaknesses, values, and emotional responses. Self-awareness allows you to see yourself clearly and objectively. However, you must not forget about your "shadow"—the unconscious parts of yourself that you've repressed or denied. I was always known for being a kind, compassionate, and agreeable person but also a chronic people-pleaser. Since my childhood, I have always put others' needs before my own. I grew up in a household where I felt that love and approval were conditional. I would receive praise when I was helpful, compliant, or good, but if I had a difference of opinion or expressed my own personal needs, desires, or feelings, I would see everyone become distant, angry, and cold towards me. They'd often say things like "she's crazy" or "what is wrong with you?" I really struggled to regulate my emotions. My dad did take me to therapy as an adolescent to try and help me identify where these emotions stemmed from. My therapist would always tell me about my "abandonment issues" due to my mother not being consistently present in my life. She claimed that consequently, I developed a yearning to just be loved and accepted. I became a "people-pleaser." I deeply feared conflict and being rejected. Over time, this fear grew into a deep-rooted subconscious belief that limited me from expressing my true emotions and asserting my needs. I thought my value was tied to how much I could please others, so once I started school and met my peers, I yearned for external validation. I felt that as long as I made everybody around me happy, I would be loved and accepted.

Of course, going unidentified and unaddressed, these traits followed me into my adult life. In relationships, I'd often sacrifice my own needs, values, and desires and found myself over-committing. I would always say yes, suppressing my own true feelings. For a long time, this was my shadow. This was the "hidden" trait I refused to acknowledge. I would constantly make excuses for horrible boyfriends, friends, and even toxic family members that I had allowed to "love bomb," manipulate, and take advantage of me. Of course, this resulted in heartbreaking results that left me even more emotional and confused. That was until I made the decision everything about my life had to change. I no longer wanted to continue to sink and be toxic. I wanted to live a peaceful life of abundance, and I desperately needed things to turn around. I started watching YouTubers who talked about business, self-development, mindset, success—anything that would reinforce that gut feeling I was meant for greater.

Initially, I thought I had money problems, but I later learned I had mindset, belief, and self-esteem problems. As I watched these videos, one common belief remained the same: mindset played a major role in all of their success. The first business I started was selling drinks, then selling candles, clothes, etc. It didn't matter; I simply became a businesswoman. However, this did not rid me of my people-pleasing and other toxic traits, so ultimately, my life remained the same. The chaos didn't subside and disappear. After all, I hadn't changed myself, my preferences, or the people I allowed to enjoy my energy. I was still living in toxicity, often using drinking, partying, and rage as my main coping mechanisms. It wasn't until I became pregnant with my son, Artist, that I became clear-minded and got this intense urge to want more and do better. I no longer wanted to live in negativity. I became fascinated with a better connection with God, healing, growing, ascending, spirituality, and becoming an even more successful businesswoman. I started learning more about people like Joe Dispenza, ET The Hip Hop Preacher, Myron Golden, and other successful people who express the importance of mindset, spirituality, and self-improvement in the journey to success. Shortly after, I found myself in "transformative therapy." This is where the real shadow work began.

As I began to explore my shadow, I uncovered my deep-rooted "fear of being seen and heard." I started to understand that the lack of awareness of my shadow had unlocked patterns of exhaustion, resentment, rage, substance abuse, and just overall toxicity. When I failed to speak up for myself and establish my own set of boundaries, I created a monster—me. I could no longer afford to keep up the facade of being "nice." I could no longer afford to sacrifice my own mental and emotional health. By acknowledging these repressed parts of myself, I was able to gain a fuller understanding of my own behaviors and identify which areas needed growth in order for me to flourish in my new identity and my new life.

So, how does one become more self-aware? Well, you can certainly start with shadow work. Shadow work is the process of uncovering and integrating the unconscious parts of yourself. It's easy for one to identify strengths/weaknesses on a more technical level when involving skill, but what really holds you back characteristically that keeps you from your full potential? These character flaws often dwell in our shadows, in the background, hidden, waiting to be discovered. These shadow elements often contain emotions, desires, and traits that in some way stunt your growth. Even though they are hidden from your unconscious mind, they continue to influence your thoughts, behaviors, and relationships. Without shadow work, your self-awareness remains incomplete. You have to be willing to see past your desirable, more positive traits and also see the darker aspects of yourself. Shadow work is fundamental to understanding exactly who you are and why you react the way you do. Most of what drives our behavior comes from our deep-rooted unconscious beliefs, fears, and desires. Shadow work brings these elements to the surface so you can address them. True self-awareness involves accepting both the light and dark sides of your personality. By acknowledging the shadow, you become aware of your flaws, insecurities, and repressed desires, allowing for a more authentic, integrated sense of self.

Identify and recognize where trauma affects your interpretation of things and your personality. Learn to love and accept all aspects of who you are. Learn to heal unresolved feelings and emotions instead of suppressing them. This unresolved emotional energy can manifest as emotional outbursts, self-sabotage, and recurring negative patterns. When I was in my people-pleasing era, I ignored my own desires and boundaries until I was so fed up I would have what I like to call rage sessions. I would yell insulting remarks and even damage others' personal property and assets. Of course, once I reacted off of my inner turmoil this way, I became seen as "crazy" or referred to as "not wrapped too tight." I had to become fully aware of these buried emotions, bring them to the forefront and release them in a way that was conducive to my growth.

When we let our shadow elements go ignored, we often project them onto others, seeing in them the qualities we can't recognize in ourselves. Shadow work helped me become aware of these projections and take responsibility for my emotions rather than blaming others for my negative feelings. It deepened my emotional intelligence and forced me to understand and confront my triggers, insecurities, and reactive behaviors. When you're aware of your shadow, you're less likely to be ruled by unconscious impulses and more likely to respond to situations with clarity and self-control. Shadow work and self-awareness both involve peeling back the real layers of who you are. Self-awareness begins with recognizing your conscious thoughts and behaviors and dives deeper into the unconscious motivations and repressed aspects of yourself. Together, they create a more authentic sense of self-awareness. You must learn to integrate shadow work with self-awareness. Journaling, mindful observations, therapy, meditation, and self-compassion can help you grow, heal, and adapt.

When journaling, reflect on your day-to-day experiences, particularly moments where you felt triggered overly emotional or judgemental. These clues will help you identify the deep shadow aspects of yourself. It's important to observe your reactions closely in situations where you feel discomfort or resentment. Ask yourself, "Can these feelings be projections of my shadow?" Utilize meditation to create a space of non-judgemental awareness where unconscious material can emerge. This will help you become more aware of those subconscious feelings and patterns.

However, remember to use grace to lead this journey. Be kind to yourself. Understand this work is deep and complicated. After all, you're becoming someone you've never been. Accept all parts of yourself without judgment and embrace your shadow, flaws, and all. Remind yourself that it's all a part of the journey. The deeper you go, the more of a champion you become. Your commitment to the inner work will set you apart, rebuild your confidence, and even reset your frequency to a higher, more positive vibration. You'll eventually develop more confidence and a more hopeful outlook on life and situations.

In my case, I worked closely with a therapist. Working closely with a therapist allowed me to have adequate support from someone who knew and understood exactly what I was going through. She also gave me uncensored guidance and created a genuine, safe space for exploring and understanding these deeper aspects of myself.

Your journey of self-awareness is incomplete without shadow work. As you confront and embrace your shadow, you become more aware of your inner complexities, leading to true self-development, mastery, and transformation. Self-awareness is essential for personal growth and contributes tremendously to building your emotional intelligence and your overall perspective on life. You must master yourself to be in control of yourself. This means letting go of any "expectations" that are not your own or beneficial for shifting into your new identity.

Ridding yourself of societal expectations is also a crucial step towards self-awareness, and it is paramount to cultivating a genuine love for yourself. Take a moment to reflect on some things you've seen on social media or even heard about from a friend that has affected what you buy, what you consider attractive, and even what you eat?! Reflect on the beliefs your family instilled. Take a moment to reflect back to your childhood. Were you encouraged to be nurturing, accommodating, or self-sacrificing? Were there forced expectations regarding appearance, education, career, or lifestyle? How did your family define success for women, and how did that shape your ambitions? Did these beliefs truly serve you and allow you to embrace your authentic self? Or did they force you to conform and develop people-pleasing tendencies? If a belief feels forced or unnatural, more than likely, the origin is not your authentic soul. Instead, it is a belief that reflects the daunting pressures of societal expectations.

Most of the things I eventually identified as "societal expectations" while on my own healing journey, I soon realized, were not my own preferences or beliefs. I soon learned that the reason I was so ambitious when it came to attending college, working extra hard in the corporate world, and believing my main responsibility as a woman was to graduate from college, get a decent job, and make just enough to live a "normal" life, actually stemmed from household expectations presented in my adolescence. Although, in the time I spent with my grandmother she was always sure to shower me with love, reassurance, and gifts. However, I always perceived it as a pity party constantly questioning why my own parents didn't give me the same praise. In my mind, I thought "she's just trying to make me feel better." Obviously, I was wrong but the lack of consistency amongst both households fed the self-doubt as I transitioned from being an only child, living with my grandmother until the age of eight, to living in a larger family dynamic with my father, where attention and affection had to be shared. As a matter of fact, up until this transition, I'd always naturally had a big personality and a radical love for myself. When expressed, I would be told I was "extra" or "obnoxious." We never had conversations about self-esteem or the importance of loving and believing in yourself. I always felt I was reprimanded for wanting attention and reassurance or being confident and 'different'. Consequently, those big feelings became self-doubt and playing small, practically trying to be invisible. Can you remember times when you celebrated yourself, or even your accomplishments, and people made controversial remarks such as "Be humble" or "You're so full of yourself"? Unfortunately, these are the scars your personality suffers from after adhering to societal expectations. Most people, especially women, have been subtly convinced to like themselves "just enough" to avoid pissing others off. It's so important to understand that a person who has been taught to value real, authentic self-love would understand and be happy to cheer you on. Reflect on how women are portrayed in the media. Think about influencers, ads, and commercials. What beauty standards or lifestyles are presented as "ideal"? Be honest: how do these portrayals affect your self-image and how you interpret your self-worth? How many times have you seen something become a trend that can actually be perceived as a sign of insecurity?

I once attended a consultation for a breast augmentation. It was at the start of my journey as a content creator. I'd just launched my clothing line and cosmetic business, Mimi's Vault. All I would see up and down my timeline were women with "perfect" boobs, butts, bodies, teeth, hair. I thought to myself, "Now, how the heck will I compete with all of these beauty influencers?" This was before my second baby, Artist, who, thankfully, gave me some more curves. After my stage of heavy drug/alcohol abuse and trauma, I'd become straight up and down skinny. I would often go down the rabbit hole of self-hate and doubt, leading me to a never-ending cycle of discouragement. Next thing I knew, I was sending a photo of my bird chest to some plastic surgeon to see how much it would cost to make me look like the beauty queens I'd seen up and down my timeline. Eventually, I decided to pour more money into building my business and revisit the implants once I actually created some cash flow. Well, Thank God I decided to heal instead. I saved myself a significant amount of money and later understood that this moment was a very significant step in empowering myself. I showed myself that God created me perfectly in his eyes, and that was greater and way more significant in the grand scheme of things. Understand that God has already stamped you!!

> *"I will praise thee; for I am fearfully and wonderfully made: Marvellous are thy works; and that my soul knoweth right well."*-PSALM 139:14 (KJV)

You don't need to look for validation from anyone or anywhere else. Your true validation comes from within. God placed love in your heart, but the world does its best to strip it away. Most of us aren't even aware of how our insecurities are being used for their benefit and to our detriment. With awareness comes a solution. Write down these observations of societal expectations so you can gain clarity on how these pressures negatively affect your life. Reflect on whether you've internalized these beliefs and whether they still serve your authentic self in the present day. Make a conscious effort to limit media that perpetuates unrealistic standards and compare how you feel when you engage with diverse, authentic representations of women. You have to take a serious inventory of your emotional triggers and identify where societal standards may be shaping your thoughts and behaviors. Journaling is an excellent tool for capturing these reflections and gaining insight into what you truly value. Embrace body positivity, self-acceptance, and diversity in yourself. Understand that you are unique and set apart. Your uniqueness is your power and what makes you YOU. Only engage with other people who genuinely love and support you, flaws and all! Be sure to have dealbreakers and boundaries so you're never in the presence of energy that makes you question your worth and value. Curate your timeline to support more women who embrace authenticity, natural beauty, and self-love.

Recognize that it's ok to break away from societal expectations and redefine beauty, success, and happiness on your own terms. Use God's word instead as the standard. Use your authentic reflection as the standard. Become intentional in making choices that reflect YOUR true desires rather than conforming to what others expect of you and succumbing to peer pressure. Constantly remind yourself that living authentically means accepting your strengths, imperfections, and weaknesses. God makes no mistakes. Focus on creating a life that feels fulfilling and meaningful to you. Nobody else has to "get it," either. After all, you're the only one who has to live YOUR life. Make yourself happy first. Erasing societal expectations and creating your own authentic values and belief system will lead to a deeper sense of self-awareness, self-acceptance, and empowerment. Getting to know yourself deeply is absolutely necessary. Deep reflection and awareness are two critical aspects of rebuilding your self-love, self-concept, and self-worth.

Some exercises that significantly contributed to my growth are:

- Journaling
- Meditation
- Isolation
- Inner Child/Shadow Work
- Self-Reflection through Relationships
- Creative Expression
- Clarifying Your Values
- Mirror Work

Journaling will allow you to externalize your thoughts and further explore your emotions, experiences, and inner turmoil. Your journal should be your personal safe space for reflection. I encourage you to get really vulnerable with yourself. The ability to sit with me and assess myself with no judgment allowed me to see what was affecting my self-concept negatively. There was nobody screaming back at me that I was "wrong," "crazy," or "complicated" for expressing myself. I was able to gain more insight into how I actually felt about myself—what affected my mood, what motivated me, and most importantly, what was holding me back.

Here are some prompts you can utilize in the upcoming weeks to encourage reflection on values, fears, desires, and personal growth.

Day 1: What activities or moments make you feel most like yourself? Why? Describe the feeling in detail.

Day 2: When do you feel most disconnected from yourself? What circumstances or people contribute to that feeling? Based on the results, are those people worthy of remaining in your life? In what ways can you replace the activities that make you feel disconnected with the moments/activities that make you feel most like yourself?

Day 3: What 3 things would you start or do today if you had no fear of judgment or failure? How can you rearrange your habits and commit more time to at least one of them?

Day 4: Are there any beliefs about yourself that you've outgrown? How can you take steps toward living in alignment with your new identity?

Day 5: Describe your most authentic self in three words. Why did you choose these words?

Day 6: What is something you've been hiding or holding back from others? What fear do you face when acknowledging it, and how can you rebuild your self-worth to be more comfortable with expressing who you are authentically, even if some people dislike you?

Day 7: What boundaries do you need to set to protect your energy and honor your authentic self? What is TRULY holding you back from setting these boundaries from this point forward?

Day 8: What things do you need to forgive yourself for in order to move forward with more self-compassion? How does identifying these things contribute to the rebuilding of your self-worth?

Day 9: When was the last time you felt truly proud of yourself? What does that say about what you value the most? If you haven't felt proud of yourself lately, how can you cultivate new habits that place you more in alignment with being proud of yourself?

Day 10: Romanticize how life looks once you fully embrace who you are without trying to meet anyone's expectations... What does a day look like in this new identity? Who are you around? How do you start your day? What habits do you have?

Writing things down, especially when it comes to your deep-rooted emotions, is significant in gaining more clarity. You may become overwhelmed or confused when a million thoughts are constantly swirling in your mind. Journaling brings those thoughts out of your head and onto paper, allowing you to see patterns and identify what you should be prioritizing. Remember, just like with anything else, consistency is key! Journaling regularly encourages a habit of self-reflection. The best part is actually being able to look back at your past journal entries over time and see the personal growth. However, just like the past is important, so is the present moment. Journaling helps ground you in the present moment, heightening mindfulness. It encourages you to slow down and engage fully with what you're feeling and kind of takes you through it but away from it at the same time.

I would lay on my bed, well really, my mattress in Philly, and just write. I would write business ideas, how much money I needed, what I wanted to accomplish, etc. In that moment, I was able to feel the feeling of disappointment in myself, but at the same time, I felt motivated and empowered because I knew the tables would turn. That little glimmer of hope continued to fuel my fire and gave me something to not only look forward to but be hopeful about. Needless to say, most of the things I wrote then, I'm living in now. So what do I do? I continue to journal constantly in pursuit of fostering a greater sense of self-compassion, embracing my imperfections, and celebrating my strengths. YOU NEED TO START JOURNALING. You must be so in tune with your own beat that nobody else's music or riff-raff affects you. Check in with yourself regularly and really be disciplined in understanding who you are, what you value, and how you can grow.

In order for you to actually check in authentically with yourself, you must know yourself. I'm not referring to the version of you that's adopted everyone else's values or principles either, obviously. I'm speaking about the version of you that existed before all the external noise and the outside pressure. From the moment we're born, we're thrown into the unknown. Along with physical development, we develop our habits, behaviors, thoughts, values, and, most importantly, our perception and mindset. If you grew up well off, with endless resources, you view the world as being abundant. You know, the glass-half-full kind of belief system. However, if you grew up in struggle, chaos, or a lack of resources, you probably naturally viewed the world with a "glass-half-empty" mindset. "We don't have money for that" or "Dreams don't pay bills" may be some of the phrases you heard often. Subconsciously, this was constantly being replayed in your mind, fostering the belief that "money doesn't come easy," and it's practically impossible to have a lot of it. That's not the case at all. The truth is, what you believe, you attract.

> *"For as he thinks in his heart, so is he."*
> PROVERBS 23:7 (KJV)

Even when considering the law of attraction, the belief is that "Thoughts become things." The core idea is that your mind is powerful, and whatever you consistently think about will eventually manifest in your reality. This means focusing on positive thoughts can attract positive outcomes, while dwelling on negativity will cause you to think negatively and most likely create a negative outcome. All those beliefs that have been forced on you are constantly swimming around in your subconscious mind. This is where centering yourself becomes extremely beneficial. Once you can identify and uproot those beliefs from your subconscious mind, you'll then be able to transform them.

Meditation allows you to break free from automatic thoughts, reactions, and beliefs that operate below your conscious awareness. Your subconscious mind holds patterns, beliefs, and habits that shape your perception based on past experiences. If the only way you can see things is, technically, through someone else's lens or agenda, are they really even your thoughts? Knowing who you are authentically is obviously monumental in becoming more self-aware. How can you fall madly in love with yourself if your mind is always in a constant battle for your life? I personally believe that this very scenario right here is the reason some of your 'manifestations' never appear. You've been praying and praying, writing things down, and nothing has changed in your reality. An essential part of manifesting is actually believing. The same thing is true as it relates to prayer. If you truly can't believe genuinely, then those manifestations are nothing more than words scribbled on paper.

"Therefore I say unto you, what things soever ye desire, when ye pray, believe that ye receive them, and ye shall have them." -MARK 11:24 (KJV)

You must believe in order to manifest. That's the magic; that's the superpower. If you were already a believer, you'd already be your "dream girl" or your "best self." Fortunately for you, not believing is not your fault. Your environment and circumstances taught you how to react, feel, and what to believe. If you were never taught to love yourself and believe in your wildest dreams, well, I guess you'd never know or BE. The whole goal of meditation is to interrupt those "automatic" patterns and create new neural pathways for better, more self-righteous thoughts. Thoughts that actually serve you and allow you to bloom. You must build your emotional resilience and reinforce positive intentions. It's time to step out of the old, unproductive cycles and build a life aligned and rooted in your truest desires.

Basic Meditation Session 101

Preparation (5 Minutes)

- **Find a quiet space:** I'd like you to find a comfortable, quiet spot where you won't be disturbed. Sit in a relaxed position with your spine straight. You can also lie down if you prefer.
- **Set Your Intentions:** Take a moment to decide what you'd like to gain from this meditation session or heart-to-heart with yourself. What do you yearn deeply to give you that feeling of being complete? What will make you the most content with your life and your conception of self? Would you like to gain inner peace, clarity, self-love, or rid yourself of a limiting belief?

Centering Yourself (5 Minutes)

- **Focus on Your Breathing:** Now, you must center yourself. Begin by taking slow, deep breaths. Inhale deeply through your nose, filling your lungs, then exhale slowly through your mouth. With each breath, imagine releasing tension and clearing away any stress or worries.
- **Calm Your Mind:** As you continue breathing, let go of any distracting thoughts. Acknowledge them and allow them to pass. Return your focus to your breath. This will help you create a sense of calm and presence.

Body Scan (5 Minutes)

- **Connect With Your Body:** Starting from the top of your head, slowly scan through your body. Go from the top down. Observe any areas of tension or discomfort.

- **Relax & Release:** As you notice each area, gently release any tension. Relax your body from head to toe. This process helps ground you in the present moment, enhancing your awareness of how you're feeling physically and emotionally.

Visualize & Connect With Your True Self (5 Minutes)

- **Imagine Your Ideal Self:** Picture yourself as the person you want to become. Visualize yourself living confidently, at peace, and free from any limiting beliefs.
- **Feel The Emotions:** Allow yourself to feel the emotions associated with this version of you—joy, fulfillment, confidence, and self-love. Let these feelings fill you, reinforcing the belief that this version of you is real and achievable.

Affirm & Reprogram Your Subconscious (5 Minutes)

- **Repeat Positive Affirmations:** Silently, or in your head, repeat these affirmations that support your growth and self-belief. Here are some powerful and intentional affirmations that will speak to your soul:
  - o My heart and mind are open to endless possibilities, and I welcome abundance in all forms.
  - o I honor my unique path and embrace my authentic self with love and compassion.
  - o Every experience I encounter serves my growth, and I trust the journey unfolding for me.

- o I release all limiting beliefs and fully step into my power, courage, and resilience.
- o I am whole, complete, and worthy of all the love, joy, and success life has to offer.

Citing these powerful affirmations consistently can help you align with a mindset of self-worth, openness, and resilience, bringing you closer to the person you aspire to be.

- **Feel the Affirmations:** Don't just repeat the words; actually, let them sink in. Genuinely feel and believe each statement as if it's already true, embedding them deeply into your subconscious mind.

Sit and Receive (5 Minutes)

- **Be Open To Inner Wisdom:** Let go of the affirmations and sit quietly. Allow any thoughts, insights, or feelings to come to you without judgment. Trust that your subconscious will offer you guidance, clarity, and a sense of peace. Stay fully present, receptive, and connected to the inner stillness. Enjoy that sense of calm and completeness.

Closing & Gratitude (5 Minutes)

- **Express Gratitude:** Gently bring your awareness back to the room and take a few deep breaths. Thank yourself for dedicating this time to self-discovery and growth.
- **Reflect On Your Intention:** Go back to the intention you set at the beginning and acknowledge any feelings or

insights that arose during your meditation session. Trust that this session has brought you closer to becoming the person you desire to be.

After this session, my hope is that you feel more relaxed and connected to your true self. I hope you feel guided toward greater self-awareness, empowerment, and peace. The more you practice, the more likely you'll create a positive, lasting impact on your mindset and wellbeing.

End Session

The sole purpose of meditation is to align your subconscious thoughts with a new belief system—a belief system that isn't tainted by society, lack of self-esteem, fear, scarcity, and all the other negative emotional connections you made through being 'let down' and your traumatic experiences. Meditation can help to erase negative thoughts and help you cultivate a more positive mindset rooted in confidence and knowing wholeheartedly who you are—knowing your true power.

In order for any of these self-building strategies to have a lasting, deep, and powerful effect, a period of isolation will not only be necessary but, in most cases, inevitable. Most people are unwilling to do this intense self-development work. This leaves them stuck in a frequency or 'understanding' that you'll eventually ascend above. As a result, your relationships may suffer and become more stressful and strained. This could possibly draw you back into a season you've already begun to uproot, like people-pleasing. When your season of isolation rears its ugly head, it's best to allow things to happen naturally. Go with the flow, and try not to force or control things.

When all of my relationships suddenly began to spiral, it lowered my vibration and motivation. I went into a sunken place, a place of guilt, shame, and embarrassment until I started to really understand that most people really live their entire lives stuck in the same unfulfilling cycle, constantly tolerating instead of creating. I had to fall back in love with myself for me to understand that my energy, my frequency, is exclusive. You must be deserving, and no, I won't feel bad about it. You chose to settle. I chose to ascend. I wish you nothing but the best but I'm on a whole different wave now, literally. You can't continue to hold onto things when you truly love yourself, especially if and when they're no longer serving you. Everything should be an even energy exchange. That way, you don't become burnt out, and you're able to pour one hundred percent into yourself. You must learn to rely solely on yourself and remove all external nuances. It may be challenging to be alone, but understand there's a huge difference between being alone and being lonely. Isolation gives you the opportunity to become your own best friend, allowing you to ALWAYS put your own affairs at the forefront. You will learn to appreciate who you are at the core. You'll strengthen your sense of self and your ability to navigate life with authenticity and insane confidence.

On this journey, I gained a deeper connection with God. Instead of trusting in people, I was forced to put all of my trust in Him. It became easier for me to hear and feel the presence of God without distractions or deterrence.

Your season of isolation is the perfect time to do your inner child/shadow work. Shadow work will be a pivotal moment in your identity transformation. Well, at least it was for me. One of the most significant characteristics that was lodged deep in my subconscious, deep in my shadow, was my prevalent people-pleasing. I presume by now you can most certainly conclude that people-pleasing was embedded deep into my DNA. There was a point in time when I literally cared more about others' feelings than I actually cared about my own. Saying "no" wasn't even in my vocabulary. I would often say "yes," knowing I would definitely regret it later. Most times, I was deep in regret the moment I said yes. Not only was my people-pleasing behavior "hidden" in my shadow, but it also became one of the most significant pieces of my inner child healing. After all, my habit of people-pleasing came as a result of my childhood.

I firmly believe that inner child healing and shadow work go hand in hand. You must first understand the purpose of the shadow work you're doing. The journey is all about growth, healing, and self-acceptance, not about self-judgment. Understanding yourself more deeply will help you become more balanced and authentic. You'll be able to move through the world with so much genuine power and clarity. Yes, you will have to plunge through a range of uncomfortable emotions and memories, but it'll be well worth it in the end. Always approach your "shadow" with self-compassion, patience, and an open mind. It's time for you to accept yourself fully, even the parts you may not be proud of.

One of the most important aspects is also identifying your triggers. What makes you feel emotions like anger, jealousy, resentment, etc? When you notice these emotions begin to fester, begin to question yourself: Why is this situation affecting me so deeply and making me feel this way? What would bring me away from this emotion without having it emerge? For example, if you start to feel jealous, ask yourself what that feeling says about your own insecurities or desires. Begin to keep track. Express and release by journaling, and transform it into positive projection. Recognize that these are actually admired traits. Understand that they are within you as well, and start to embrace those traits within yourself. Shadow work also involves journaling/documenting, meditation, and deep reflective questioning. To be extremely clear, this is how your self-paced shadow work journaling should look:

Informal Self-Paced Shadow Work Sesh

Step 1: Set the Scene

- **Get Cozy:** Find a comfortable spot where you can relax without any interruptions. You can even light a candle, play soft music, or make a cup of tea—whatever helps you feel the most at ease.

- **Set A Light Intention:** What insight do you wish to gain from this shadow work? Some examples are "I want to minimize the number of times I become angry/agitated throughout the day" or "I'm open to exploring any hidden parts of myself."

Step 2: Current Mood Check-In

- **Ask yourself:** "How am I feeling right now?" Don't overthink. Just jot down the first words that come to mind, like "tired," "excited," "anxious," "curious," etc.

- **Follow Up:** What feelings stood out to you? Dig deeper into that. For example, if you're feeling anxious, ask yourself, "What's in the back of my mind making me feel this way?"

Step 3: Reflect

- **Think of a recent reaction:** Reflect on a moment recently when you felt a strong reaction to something or someone. For example, has something made you angry, agitated, irritated, etc., lately? It's important to be completely honest with yourself. Even if the reaction didn't cause a scene, the internal reactions are the ones that need to be acknowledged the most in this scenario. Those are the feelings that desperately need to surface and be purged.

- **Purge:** WRITE IT DOWN. In detail, describe what exactly happened and how it made you feel.
- **Get Real:** Take a moment to reflect on WHY this interaction made you feel this way. Sometimes, the answer is right there; other times, it may take a little digging. If you don't know right away, that's okay. Just let it sit! Revisit this entry later.

Step 4: Deep-Seeded Self Reflection

- **Self-Reflection Prompts:** What am I afraid people might see in me? What's something I don't like admitting about myself? What traits in other people do I judge or dislike? Why? Are there times when I project my inner insecurities negatively onto others?

  Side Note: Please remember these answers are for your eyes only. There is no need to be ashamed or afraid of understanding yourself on a deeper level. Remember, this work is only going to make you into a better, more divine, more confident version of yourself. This work is meant to help you, not harm or "expose" you. Trust yourself and trust the process.

- **Flip The Script:** Choose one thing you wrote that makes you feel "uncomfortable" or negatively. Instead of instantly judging yourself, ask yourself, "What could this part of me need or want?" "What could this be teaching me?" "What can I do to help/refrain from using the undesired behavior in the next situation?"

- **Uproot & Re-Examine:** Think more about these negative traits you've written/reflected on. How have these traits actually helped you? Let me explain: Sometimes, our negative traits actually serve a purpose or have protected us in some way. For example, maybe your "stubbornness" has helped you stand up for yourself. Or maybe your "cockiness" keeps you from low-quality experiences. Your rationale doesn't have to "make sense," but dig deep for the answer. Try hard to see the whole picture.

Step 5: Give Yourself Love & Grace

- **End with an Intention:** Close this intimate session by writing down something that makes you feel empowered and connects with your subconscious to make you feel supported on this meaningful journey!!

"I am committed to accepting and loving myself exactly as I am."

"I am gentle with myself, especially during times of change and growth."

"I embrace all of my imperfections, knowing they make me unique and beautiful."

In this moment, it's so important to release any feelings of guilt or embarrassment. Understand that nobody is perfect and everything can be altered. You create your reality. Do what makes you feel empowered.

End Session

There are many different ways to do shadow work. My hope is that you execute it in a way that is meaningful to you—a way that truly frees you and cultivates growth in the areas that hold you back from being one hundred percent submerged in your new identity. You know, BIG CONFIDENCE. The point is to make you feel more comfortable with understanding that while you may not be perfect, you are worthy and highly qualified to pop your sh*t! Period.

As you transition from isolation back out to the outer world, you may notice some strains in your close and intimate relationships, friendships, etc. For me, it came all too soon and way too abruptly. I honestly believe this was one of the most painful seasons in my growth journey. It's hard to create distance between you and the people you love the most, but I also find it to be very necessary. People have already formed their ideals of you in their eyes, and a lot won't be willing to change their perception no matter how hard you try to "prove it" or live your natural "new" life. They'll believe it's a facade and sometimes even downplay you. Once you start hearing comments like "What you think you better than everybody" or "You changed," then you know you've entered a new era.

Now, it's time to do some self-reflection through relationships. Like with shadow work, we have to dig deeper into our relationships and make some hard decisions based on our findings. When I took a close look at a lot of my relationships, I noticed I was overextending, people-pleasing (of course), shrinking myself, and sometimes just being plain old naive. I had to be truthful with myself and admit that I was the reason for the misalignments. I paid close attention to how I was reacting emotionally, subconsciously, and physically in each and every situation. Strong emotions, whether positive or negative, can reveal hidden beliefs, triggers, and unresolved issues within yourself. If you find yourself in a situation that you're triggered by, just like with shadow work, you must dissect and assess. Look for recurring patterns in your behavior with certain people or energies around you. Do you tend to feel the same way in certain situations, people, or places? Are there similar issues that come up across multiple relationships? When finding yourself in an unwanted conflict, conversation, or environment, try to listen deeply to others instead of focusing on what you'll say next. Listening allows you to see how you may project your thoughts, assumptions, or insecurities onto them. It also allows you to understand their logic or thought process a little more and decide if they even truly align with you and your values. When you go through the process of healing, growing, and becoming more enlightened, you will start to become more aware and vibrate at a higher frequency. You'll notice that those who refuse to do the work may vibrate at a lower frequency. Those people keep scarcity and a closed mindset at the forefront. Remember we talked about the "force-feeding" of scare tactics and fixed mindsets by your parents, upbringing, environments, and society?! Well, most people never prioritize this deep inner work, leaving them in a never-ending whirlwind of unwarranted emotions and an unfulfilling, low-frequency life in general. Luckily for you, you aren't those people. The fact that you took the time to purchase this book shows that you are already escaping the trap and executing the strategies. Becoming the higher frequency will finish the job.

Understand this is a life-long journey, not a destination. Better will begin to flow to you naturally. Each time, you'll raise the bar yet again. It's so important to protect your energy (your energetic frequency). Robert Greene's book "The 48 Laws of Power" talks about this concept. Specifically, law 10: "Infection: Avoid the Unhappy & Unlucky." This law advises that associating with individuals who are perpetually unhappy or unlucky can negatively influence your own life, as their negative energy and misfortune may spread to you. This could only mean that the other extreme is also true. Surrounding yourself with positive and successful people can lead to shared good fortune and happiness. It's so important not to avoid the red flags the first time. Personally, that was one of my greatest mistakes. I would often get a gut feeling about something and ignore it, thinking that I was in control of the outcome or I could make that person better. Here's the reality: all you can control is you. The assignment is you. The same way you audit your own behaviors is the same way you should assess the energy you allow into your space. Some refer to this gut feeling as 'discernment.' Whatever term works for you is ok; just make sure you are watering yourself so you can feel and see when things are counterfeit. The deeper you slip into awareness of yourself and spirituality, the more you'll be able to feel or discern things that you've surpassed and outgrown. Don't delay. Simply detach at the first sign of turmoil. You've come too far to allow yourself to shrink or return to a chaotic frequency. You must allow yourself to detach without feeling "bad" about it. It's time to finally put yourself first—unapologetically.

The law of detachment is a principle often found in spiritual, psychological, and self-development teachings. In order to manifest or achieve something, you must release your need to control or cling to a specific outcome. It's all about having a goal or desire but allowing space for God to work in ways that may be unexpected. In other words, trust the process and have faith in your ability to handle whatever unfolds, even if things don't quite match your vision right away. Set your intentions, and know that everything is unfolding in alignment with your divine destiny. When I got that devastating news about my uncle, I didn't allow it to scare me into remaining comfortable. I instead packed my belongings and prepared myself for the ride of my life. I knew that I, with God's help, could and would make a way. If you are meant to remain in an era of your life, you will. If people are meant to stay, they will. You don't have to "force." Take a step back from the need to have control. Continue to grow yourself, and everything will unfold just as it should.

You begin to become more objective and more seasoned in recognizing patterns and beliefs that may not serve your growth. When you aren't so attached to the outcome or your own expectations, you can see things more clearly. I had to stop excusing others' behavior and blaming myself. When my relationships continued to fail, I had to detach and let go of my ego to truly open my eyes. I began to see people as who they were and not who I expected them to be, thus allowing me to really see myself as who I was becoming and not who I used to be. Not only is it important to detach from others, but detachment allows you to disconnect yourself from the overbearing expectations you may have created in your very own mind. The struggle was real when I turned 30. I kept getting this relentless feeling that I should have been much further in life, especially in regard to my entrepreneurship journey. I was still holding on to resentment and was extremely bitter about not being what I saw as "ahead in life." I blamed my parents, I blamed my circumstances, and mostly, I blamed myself. "Why didn't I learn these things sooner?" "Why did I waste so much of my life on bullsh*t?" These questions constantly haunted me. The what-ifs and why didn't I's drove me completely insane. Detachment means becoming less and less tied to the stories your ego creates about who you "should be," how you think things should turn out, and how others "ought" to perceive you. I had to free myself from external validation and detach from the outcome completely. I now choose to remain rooted in the now, knowing that I was becoming somebody I'd never been.

TRUST. It's very important to lean into that. And I mean genuine trust. Not just the monotone idea of saying you trust but actually feeling, believing, and knowing energetically. Directly after this comes execution. Does this thought, feeling, or atmosphere make sense for where I am or where I'm headed? Tap into your awareness, identify, and detach.

Well, my friend, that concludes the segment on peeling back the layers and meeting the fabulous, flawed, fearless you underneath. Self-awareness and your inner ideal concept not only allow you to live your life authentically but also build confidence in your uniqueness, fostering an environment where you can truly begin to unleash your inner divine power.

Dear Me,

Today, I want to take a moment to recognize the incredible journey I'm on—a journey that has led me to face not only the bright, joyful parts of myself but also the shadows. I'm learning daily to embrace every part of me with love and compassion, knowing that each layer, each hidden part, holds a truth I need to understand. I understand that this work may not be easy, but it's necessary and liberating. I'm dedicated to diving deeper, peeling back the layers, and facing my fears, insecurities, and doubts. I know that those things don't define me; they're simply parts of my story that I'm ready to rewrite. I am stepping away from the constraints of society, releasing the weight of expectations and judgments that don't align with who I truly am. I am no longer concerned with fitting in. Instead, I'm committed to carving my own path rooted in my values, my dreams, and my authenticity. I know that becoming the best version of myself doesn't come from following the crowd; it comes from looking within, listening to my own voice, and trusting my inner wisdom. Every day, I grow more connected to THE REAL ME, the most authentic and transparent version of me. I am powerful, resilient, and wise. I know my worth is not dictated by the world but defined by my own radical self-love and acceptance. I am grateful for the courage to face my shadow, the clarity to see myself as I am, and the strength to let go of what no longer serves me. I understand that in doing so, I am creating space for joy, abundance, and purpose to flow freely into my life. This journey is my gift to myself. It's my commitment to becoming the woman I've always dreamed of being, one who stands in her power and inspires other women to do the same. I lead by example. I am becoming whole, rooted in love, and unshakably aligned with my truth. I am so, so proud of me.

With endless love and gratitude,
ME

CHAPTER 2

Breaking The Funhouse Mirror
Dispelling Self-Doubt

∞

"The most dangerous lies are the ones we tell ourselves."
-RICHARD BACH

Close your eyes and imagine standing in front of a fun house mirror. Picture a twisted reflection that warps your image, exaggerating flaws and distorting every angle until you barely recognize yourself. This is the same effect self-doubt and insecurity have on our minds. We trick ourselves into believing we're less capable, less beautiful, and less worthy than we truly are. Just like the funhouse mirror, these beliefs are not real. These are merely reflections born from past experiences, beliefs, and cultural expectations that we've internalized, often without question. In this chapter, I invite you to step away from that distorted image and uncover THE TRUTH.

First, understand that NOTHING is wrong with you for thinking this way. I used to blame and down-talk myself for being insecure and doubtful, often thinking, "Why am I so weird?" or "How could I be so stupid?" Self-doubt and insecurity alter the way you perceive yourself and create an entirely different identity. To break the funhouse mirror, we must realize that these are learned behaviors rooted in early adolescent experiences, societal pressures, and the false expectations we impose on ourselves. Understanding where these thoughts come from gives us more power to dismantle these beliefs, piece by piece. We need to silence that inner critic once and for all. You have to rewire how you speak to and about yourself. Replace the harsh judgments with empowering affirmations that tell a new story. Use "I am" statements that empower the confident, capable, and resilient person you truly are. In shattering this mirror of self-doubt, you aren't just confronting your insecurities; you're reclaiming your true reflection—the reflection that cultivated your true potential, strength, and beauty.

Self-doubt and insecurity are learned responses and can be unlearned. I'm a living testimony. This is why shadow work and self-awareness are so important. Once you become empowered in who you are, it'll be easier to do away with self-doubt. If I were a product of my environment, upbringing, society, etc, you would not be reading this book by me today. If I had never had that 'aha' moment that helped me understand it was never too late to re-invent myself, I would never have been able to put 'author' in front of my name. I knew there was more to me; I had a burning desire to be more. Statistics would say that I'd end up like my parents, either trapped in the streets or overworked, undervalued, and underpaid, allowing others' thoughts/beliefs to determine my capabilities. By understanding where these negative emotions stem from, you gain the power to not only challenge but to change these beliefs. You begin to rid yourself of the false narratives you created out of scarcity and the innate need to feel accepted and validated. It's time to make space for healthier self-talk and a more supportive self-image, which will ultimately lead to an explosion of confidence. You need this confidence to embark on the road least traveled, becoming that one percent.

Key factors that have contributed to your negative self-image are:

- Your childhood experiences
- Social Comparisons and Expectations
- Fear of Failure/Rejection
- Perfectionism
- Negative Self-Talk & Inner Critic
- Trauma & Adverse Experiences

Each of these helped shape your perception or lack thereof. Early life experiences, particularly interactions with caregivers, teachers, and peers, play a significant role in shaping your mind's reality. If you, like me, faced constant criticism from your parent(s), siblings, or peers, you've unconsciously learned to internalize beliefs that you're not good enough and/or unworthy of love and acceptance. Have you ever heard the saying, "People will only do what you allow"? Well, that's actually pretty true. Think highly of yourself. Your self-concept, or how you see yourself, truly shapes the identity you create, determining the kind of life you build or accept. Society and culture set high expectations around success, appearance, and behavior. In fact, society is a major contributor to setting the standard for what "success" means and/or looks like. I took an entire class on this in college called "Mass Media." Mass media refers to the various platforms and technologies used to communicate and distribute information, news, entertainment, and advertisements to large audiences simultaneously. Nowadays, social media is massive in spreading information or what I like to call creating "collective opinions" or "group think." These media platforms influence everybody to think the same and have the same values, principles, opinions, etc.

When I first started out in entrepreneurship, using social media to broadcast my business, I would often compare myself to curated images of others, mostly beauty influencers. This only led me down the rabbit hole of feeling inadequate and not believing in myself. Think of times you may have opened your Instagram app and seen what seemed to be a perfect girl with a perfect life, and it made you start to internalize feelings of regret, incompetence, and doubt. You start to think to yourself, "Why can't I be as successful as her?" or "I wish I had a man like that, a car like that, or a life like that," when in reality, you absolutely can. Instead of taking those feelings and using them as fuel for inspiration, you start to create false narratives, which creates false fear. Fear of rejection, failure, and mistakes with no supporting evidence except your very own made-up conclusions. Fear is defined as an emotional response to a perceived threat or danger. The key word is "perceived." It's all about your perception. Really, to me, failure does not exist. You are the one who creates the standard. For example, If I start a business and spend an insane amount of money but don't get as many orders as I thought I would, would that be considered failing? What premise did I use to "create" this standard? Did I base this premise on what I perceive to be success in somebody else's reality? Fear conditions the mind to doubt one's own capabilities in order to protect one's ego from feelings of disappointment, future pain, and "embarrassment." I like to refer to fear as (f)alse (e)vidence (a)ppearing (r)eal. Failure, embarrassment—none of it truly exists unless we allow it to. You must stop falling for this unrealistic idea of perfectionism that's constantly being force-fed to you. Many women develop perfectionist tendencies as a way to gain what they see as "approval" and avoid criticism. When in reality, it is truly impossible to avoid criticism. You have to understand that whether people hate you or love you has everything to do with them and nothing to do with you. It's called projection.

Of course, you should be genuine and cultivate a magnetic, welcoming energy, but you also don't need validation from anybody but yourself and God. Being genuine and allowing your authenticity to flow will not only decrease your stress levels, but you'll no longer be "trying too hard." Using this standard, you'll attract a genuine tribe of supporters that uplift, empower, and reciprocate your abundant energy.

When you constantly set ridiculous expectations for yourself, you'll eventually begin to feel like you're always falling short. You'll begin fostering insecurities instead of promoting growth. Over time, you'll start to internalize the negative messages you've heard over and over again, reinforcing doubt. Not to mention, the traumatic experiences we go through, such as bullying, abuse, and significant loss, create lasting emotional scars. If we don't make it a point to become more aware, we distort our own reality just like the fun-house mirror. The only way to bring an end to this distorted, stagnant reality or perception is by silencing that inner critic. From now on, whenever you notice negative thoughts forming, you can mentally say "STOP." Say it aloud even. The important thing is becoming intentional about actually saying it each and every time you have those thoughts or feel those doubts. The goal is to redirect the thought and form a new thinking cycle. Research suggests we have between 6,000 to 70,000 thoughts per day. A significant portion of these thoughts tend to be repetitive and/or focused on familiar themes. Psychologists estimate that around 80% are often negative or self-critical. Of course, if you've always thought along the lines of self-doubt, scarcity, and lack due to the trauma you've encountered, then those thoughts own your mind. They become repetitive. This is why practices like affirmations, shadow work, and grounding can be so impactful; they help us shift our mindset away from those unproductive thinking patterns. You should start using a "rebuttal letter" to counter or "fight" this negative thought pattern. Simply write down a specific criticism your inner critic often whispers and then write a rebuttal as if you were defending yourself to someone else. Doing this will not only show you how utterly ridiculous you sound but also how extremely critical you are of yourself! I used to beat myself down with my own thoughts. I was my own worst critic. I'm truly creative at heart. I would think of clever branding ideas, reels to post, or videos to create, but I would often discourage myself from posting or allow doubt to stop me from taking action. I started increasing my self-concept and recognizing the vicious thought patterns that were haunting me. I was being way too hard on myself. I was allowing my own daunting belief system to trick me out of my own spot. It's so important to be extremely honest with yourself. You can't fix what you don't first become aware of. But it is also important to have balance. The moment I ended the pattern of downing myself and instead cultivated a pattern of speaking life into myself, my life became better. I had to really lock in on my goals and achieve them. Once I started meeting deadlines and achieving small goals, I created larger ones. Each goal I achieved fueled my fire even more, giving me the momentum to keep going. I was able to attract an aligned tribe of supporters and clients. Overall, life just got better. It felt better. I felt better. When you find yourself spiraling with these same negative thoughts, don't start beating yourself up. Instead, big yourself up! Practice self-compassion throughout the day, especially after mistakes or challenges. Pause to acknowledge your feelings with compassion. Place your hand on your heart, take deep breaths, and remind yourself that it's ok to be imperfect. God made you just the way you needed to be, and He loves you just the way you are. Anybody who can't see that you are fearfully and wonderfully made is a fool and isn't privy to your relationship with God and the assignment he has for your life—the assignment you were beautifully crafted by the creator to fulfill. Did I mention that God created you in His very image?!

"And God said, let us make man in our image, and after our likeness: and let them have dominion over the fish of the sea, and over the fowl of the air, and over the cattle, and all over the earth, and over every creeping thing that creepeth upon earth. So God created man in his own image, in the image of God created he him; male and female created he them."-**Genesis 1:26-27 (KJV)**

You were strategically created by God, with and for a purpose. Understanding this verse from the Bible calls us to live in a way that honors God. Most people depend solely on the verses in the bible and seem to forget about the worth we have ourselves, the inner divinity that God strategically placed in us. We can mirror the love God placed in us, but you gotta have love to give love! Work vigilantly to adopt a growth mindset response system with your thoughts. Doing this will enhance your self-concept. When your inner critic points out a flaw or failure, consciously reframe it as an opportunity to grow. Consistently remind yourself of this inner power you possess that God blessed you with. Instead of allowing negative situations to consume you, ask yourself, "What can I learn from this?" or "How can this situation make me stronger?" This shift from criticism to curiosity helps you see mistakes as part of the learning process rather than personal flaws. Disconnect your emotions from any negative feelings or thoughts and quickly respond with the alternative. Develop a mantra for the more difficult moments. Choose a phrase that resonates with you, like " I am enough" or "I am worthy of love and kindness." My thoughts really used to control me, sometimes taking control of my whole day and plummeting my energy and motivation into the ground. They'd completely taken over my reality, causing frequent anxious spirals and bouts of "depression." Little did I know, I'd manifested those horrible things into my reality. Remember: You get what you think about. I would often succumb to negative, obsessive thoughts like "Everybody is so fake," "Nobody really likes me; they don't even like my pictures," and "My family hates me; they've never supported me." Regardless of whether these things were actually "true" or figments of my perception, I allowed them to become true in my reality. I was constantly allowing myself to think in a negative, low-frequency pattern. I utilized visualization to begin shifting my focus.

When your inner critic is loud, close your eyes and visualize a place that makes you feel safe and calm—a beach, forest, or cozy room. Imagine the voice fading as you immerse yourself in this setting. Alternatively, you could imagine a beautiful moment with your kids or a moment you were being celebrated and extremely proud of yourself. This visualization will help redirect your mind to a space of peace and silence the negativity. You'll also start to transition your subconscious mind from negative thinking patterns to more positive thinking, resulting in your vibration being on a higher frequency. Physical movements like a brisk walk, yoga, or even just a light stretch can help release tension and raise your frequency as well. Each day, commit to doing something kind for yourself that counters your inner critic's narrative. These small acts of self-love reaffirm your value and drown out self-doubt. Over time, you will build resilience against your inner critic and foster a more compassionate and positive relationship with yourself. The absolute best and most influential part is your affirmations. Positive and specific affirmations will not only change how you feel about yourself but also change the directives your subconscious mind sends to your conscious mind to make you feel that way.

Remember, earlier in the text, we talked about how your subconscious mind is like a storehouse. It sends signals about how you feel or how you react. Your subconscious mind is comprised of your good and bad experiences, also known as your trauma. Your subconscious mind can't tell the difference between an actual, live, in-the-moment threat and a potential threat. For example, sometimes, when you just think about something horrible happening to you, you'll feel it in your body as if it is actually happening. Or you might often daydream back into your past. You'll feel that same "knot in the stomach" feeling you felt when it happened. This is why the rewiring of your subconscious mind is so important. When you're consistently saying affirmations that are tailored just for you to address your "weaknesses," you are telling your subconscious mind there is no longer a threat, and you want to vibrate on a more calm, peaceful frequency. You'll start to remind yourself of your potential and your power. With that will come empowerment beyond measure, forcing you to take actions that will continue to keep you vibrating on that frequency. When I was taking those long walks from Cecil B. Moore to Broad Street, I didn't complain. I would instead motivate myself with uplifting thoughts like, "I know this hard work will pay off soon," and "This is my right now, not my forever." I would even look forward to little things like knowing that my son would be smiling when I brought Wendy's home. I found things to be happy about, even though my world was falling apart.

Create affirmation cards with positive statements that counter your most common self-criticisms or feelings of anxiety. When you find yourself feeling low, raise your vibration by thinking about something you're grateful for and write it down. I used to get an insane amount of anxiety when it was time to attend events, gatherings, parties, etc. Really, any time I was going to be with a group of people or even just one other person, I would find myself filling a "to-go" cup with wine or liquor to "curb" that anxious feeling. Consuming the liquor, of course, in the moment, I became more at ease but extremely dependent on alcohol. Eventually, I became self-aware enough to understand that I didn't have social anxiety; I simply went through so many traumatic experiences with people that I developed a negative form of thought patterns from being around people. I was using the "tipsy" feeling to suppress the anxious feeling that stemmed from me trying to "control" or prevent myself from being hurt again. It was an extremely toxic cycle that almost landed me in Alcoholics Anonymous. Once I identified this as a trauma, I began rebuilding my confidence. I would look directly in the mirror and speak life into myself, saying these powerful affirmations aloud:

> *"I am worthy, resilient, and capable of creating the life of my dreams."*
> *"I release the need for approval from others."*
> *"I choose to focus on progress, not perfection, and I understand that."*
> *"Mistakes are opportunities for learning and growth."*

These statements are very specific and intentional. Allow your creativity and struggles to lead you in cultivating a series of statements specifically tailored and intentional for you. If you feel resistance, start by using the ones I provided and ease your way into more personalized statements. Communicate your awareness of your flaws, but also remind yourself of your power. The goal is to redirect but also create urgency for NEW actions that, in return, create new thought patterns, causing new habits to be formed. It may feel "cringe" at first, and you might not even believe what you're saying. Still, you must not let that discourage you, not just in that moment but throughout the day, as you notice your mood shifting to a lower frequency or realize you are becoming frustrated by an inconvenience. You must also embody exactly what you're reciting. When you say "I am worthy," actually cultivate that feeling of worthiness. Think about a special moment in your life that reminds you of that *worthy* feeling. If you stay consistent and intentional, you'll begin to raise your frequency and become better at keeping your frequency high.

Dear Me,

It's time to let go. Self-doubt has lingered far too long, whispering lies that I've mistakenly believed until now. Today, I'm drawing a line. I choose to reclaim my power and decide, once and for all, that I am more than enough. Self-doubt has no place in my story. It does not define me, nor will I allow it to break me. I've already overcome so much. I've faced challenges that could've broken me, yet here I am, stronger, wiser, and still standing. I proclaim this as proof of my resilience, strength, and undeniable worth. When doubt says I'm not ready, I will remind myself of all the times I took a leap, despite the presence of fear, and I landed exactly where I was meant to be. When doubt says I'm not good enough, I will counter it with the truth: I am constantly growing, learning, and becoming. When doubt says, 'What if you fail?' I will respond with, 'But what if I soar?' I recognize that self-doubt thrives on fear, but fear is nothing more than a shadow. I possess the light within to dissolve it. I vow to only focus on my gifts, my purpose, and my journey. I trust myself, I trust my instincts, I trust my capabilities, and I trust my vision. I was created by God for a reason, and my existence is already proof that I am worthy. From this moment on, every time doubt arises, I will let it remind me to rise higher. I will use it as fuel to take action, step outside of my comfort zone, and prove to myself just how unstoppable I really am. I declare that this will be the spark that ignites my courage and not the chain that holds me back. The time has come to stop questioning myself and start believing in all that I am. I don't need permission to succeed, to dream, or to become. God already gave me everything I need inside of me. No more shrinking, no more second-guessing, and no more dimming my light. I am done with self-doubt. It has no power here anymore.

With unwavering love and faith,

ME

CHAPTER 3

The Mirror of Truth

Embracing Your Flaws

∞

Listen, your so-called 'flaws' are actually superpowers. I know firsthand that accepting yourself, and I mean ALL OF YOURSELF, is not an easy task. If we don't embrace our flaws, then we'll always be incapable of reaching our full potential. The time has come for us to embody the insane confidence necessary to become the woman of our dreams. We will no longer allow these so-called "flaws" to hinder us. When I was young, I'd often hear things like, "Be quiet," "Why are you always so loud," or "Why do you have to be so obnoxious?" I used to really struggle with my sense of self and self-expression. I'd be so careful not to "say too much" or "be too extra." My self-concept was completely distorted. I was unable to see the power in being loud, opinionated, and an out-of-the-box thinker. It's unfortunate that we are often critiqued before we even understand who we truly are. Instead, we grow into who we learned to be to protect ourselves. We suppress our true identity before we have the chance to actually flourish authentically. We create negative connotations with ourselves that are actually projections from people who fail to embrace their own flaws, leading us into such a vicious, toxic, limiting cycle.

A real champion is able to identify their own flaws but also tweak them and make them work in their favor. Oprah Winfrey, for example, has always been very open about her challenging upbringing. She was raised in poverty and abuse and had a troubled childhood. Early on in her career, she was told that her background and appearance didn't fit the stereotypical mold for TV. Instead of Oprah hiding her past or trying to force herself to fit others' expectations, Oprah leaned into her authenticity, identifying that her story didn't make her incompetent or weak; it made her unique. Her unique story allowed her to connect genuinely with audiences and ask the tough, compassionate questions that set her apart in media. Her "flaws" of vulnerability and emotional depth became her biggest assets, making her one of the most influential figures in television history. She is now one of the wealthiest women in the world. Lizzo, a Grammy-winning musician, often faced criticism and scrutiny over her body size throughout her career. Instead of conforming to industry pressures to lose weight or hide her body, she embraced her physique. She made body positivity and self-love a major value in her brand. Her music and persona now celebrate self-confidence, joy, and acceptance. Lizzo has helped to redefine beauty standards in the music industry and empowered others to embrace their bodies as they are. The same thing people saw as a "flaw" has transformed Lizzo and her brand into a source of inspiration and strength for millions of women. This is solid proof that authenticity and resilience are true assets, no matter what anyone else says or thinks. These "flaws" are socially constructed. We defeat the odds by embracing them and empowering ourselves and others in the process. Write down three traits that you perceive as flaws and explore ways they could be flipped into sources of strength. Many of us grew up internalizing expectations around beauty, behavior, and success. As you write these flaws down, try hard to identify their origin. You'll soon find that you didn't even draw these conclusions about yourself, and most times, they're not even "flaws"; they are simply attributes and experiences that make you unique.

We are not here in this world to fit a generalized mold. Embracing your flaws will cause a shift in your mindset that empowers you to embrace the very qualities that society might label as flaws. Become intentional in breeding a strong sense of self-acceptance and self-confidence. You must learn to cultivate your "main character energy." Your flow of consciousness for embracing your flaws should go from becoming aware of them (shadow work) to accepting them and, finally, appreciating them. Embracing gratitude is also such an underrated growth strategy. Create a habit of consistently expressing what you're grateful for instead of complaining. Cultivate an appreciation for your own individuality and creativity. Nothing is by mistake; you were created in God's image, and you are exactly how God intended you to be. You are perfectly imperfect and in need of nothing else.

Kintsugi is a form of Japanese art that means "golden joinery." This art form stems from a beautiful philosophy that involves repairing broken pottery with lacquer-dusted or mixed with powdered gold, silver, or platinum. Instead of hiding the cracks or trying to make the piece look as it did before, Kintsugi highlights these fractures, celebrating the pottery's unique history and the beauty of its imperfections. This philosophy is a reminder that flaws and experiences shape who we are, making us much more valuable and unique. Rather than seeing brokenness as something to be hidden or discarded, it treats the cracks in the pottery as a vital part of the object's character, hence turning the cracks into a superpower and making the pottery even more unique and valuable. Kintsugi symbolizes resilience. It shows that even after being broken, something can be transformed and reborn into something new and even more beautiful.

Even after hardship or trauma, we can heal and emerge stronger and even more beautiful, making a huge impact on other people just like us. Become committed to expressing a deep level of self-compassion. Speak to yourself kindly and forgive yourself for your past mistakes. It's time to let yourself off the hook! Remind yourself that time has passed and the idea of "being perfect" does not exist. Every minute is a new chance to change your entire reality. Thoughts and feelings from the past are nothing more than tests from God to see if you're truly ready to transcend into your new identity and purposeful living. Don't overthink or react at all. Simply raise your frequency by focusing your energy on all of the good things in your current reality. Reflect on all the things you used to worry about and remember that you made it through anyway. This can and will instantly raise your frequency, reminding you of your power. Be grateful for your mind, body, and spirit and all they do to contribute to your growth and sense of self. Focus on what you can control and work on improving aspects that you actually care about. Let go of the need to change or control everything. Only spend time with those who love and accept you as you are, and stay far away from people or places that emphasize "perfectionism" or negativity. Before you know it, you'll notice yourself becoming a force to be reckoned with who doesn't care what "normal" looks like. You'll be too busy being you.

From this point forward, make a pact with yourself to make only choices that align with YOUR true values and goals. Regardless of your financial situation, what others think or feel, and societal expectations. In a world where we are constantly bombarded by messages of who we should be, be who your spirit tells you to be and commit to showing up as yourself. That's it. Do what makes your soul smile, and constantly remind yourself of your goddess energy and irresistible frequency.

Dear Me,

I know I've been hard on you. For so long, I've picked apart every flaw, magnifying them in my mind until they felt impossible to bear. I've compared you to others, wishing you could be more like them and less like you, and for that, I am deeply sorry. The truth is, those flaws I've been so quick to hide or fix are not weaknesses. These are parts of me that tell my authentic, unique story that will soon be used as a testimonial to my victory. Every scar, every misstep, every so-called imperfection has shaped the person staring back at me now. I am beautiful, not in spite of those things but because of them. Today, I choose to see myself differently. I choose to love my crooked edges, rough spots, and the cracks where the light shines through, reminding myself daily that I never needed to be perfect to be worthy. From this day forward, I promise to honor myself wholeheartedly—not just the parts of me I find easy to love, but every single part of me. I vow to regard myself with an absurd amount of compassion throughout this journey. I will constantly remind myself that the mirror doesn't reflect a project to fix but a relentless soul to celebrate. Thank you for being strong. Thank you for being you. I am proud and honored to be me, flaws and all.

With endless love and gratitude,

ME

CHAPTER 4:

Nourishing Your Reflection

Feeding Your Mind, Body and Soul

∞

"What? know ye not that your body is the temple of the Holy ghost which is in you, which ye have of God, and ye are not your own? -1 CORINTHIANS 6:19(KJV)

After the sudden passing of Lamont, things obviously got hard. Scratch that things didn't get just "hard"; things got horrible, pathetic, and unmanageable. I really felt like I was soul-less. Not only was I ripping and running the streets, I was traumatizing my body. I would go days without eating, binging instead on alcohol and ecstasy. I didn't notice this at the time, but as I reflect, I can recognize that my frequency was extremely low.

Nowadays, when I think, I also feel. Everything is a feeling. I've become very in tune with my mind, body, and soul. Therefore, my policy is if it doesn't feel right, I refuse to commit to it. Easy said, but explaining it to others is the hard part. I'm often met with resistance and a sequence of questioning like "Why though, what's your reason?" or "You have to have a reason," when actually, I don't. It just doesn't feel right is a valid enough excuse and you should never allow anyone to tell you any different. This is why it's so important to not only nourish your mind but your body and soul, too. You must navigate this world as a divine being. You'll be unable to do that if your mind, body, and soul are not in tune and full of waste. It's also impossible if you're constantly lowering your frequency and surrounding yourself with energy drainers.

My pregnancy with my son, Artist, led me to an epiphany. The fact is, with him dwelling in my womb, I was unable to partake in drugs, drinking, etc. The discipline of having to be mindful of my intake, my diet, etc, benefited me tremendously. My entire first trimester, I was too sick to eat anything heavy, like beef. I'd given up pork in 2014 when I became Muslim. I'd often consume things like fruit and veggies, and I was immensely addicted to salmon. Side Note: In the present day, I actually still love and prefer fruits, veggies, and salmon over anything else. The point is that my pregnancy detoxed my mind, body, and soul. It allowed me to re-nourish myself to health. I became more purposeful, mindful, and connected to myself. Everyone, especially in 2024, knows how important it is to nourish your body and eat 'clean' or 'healthy' food. But nobody really talks about how it's actually the origin of a total mind and soul transformation. Once my body was clear of all the trash food, I was able to think more clearly. Once I was able to think more clearly, everything else followed. I gained mental clarity, making way for higher thinking. I also learned about the gut-brain connection. The gut microbiome (trillions of microorganisms that live in your digestive tract) directly impact your mental health through the gut-brain axis. A disrupted gut microbiome can impair serotonin production, which largely occurs in the gut. Too much serotonin causes adverse effects like mood swings, difficulty concentrating, brain fog, hyperactivity, and even anxiety. Therefore, what you consume literally can change how you think, consequently altering how you feel. So, how do you start to support a healthy gut microbiome?

- **Eat a diverse, fiber-rich diet**- include a variety of fruits, vegetables, whole grains, and nuts to feed beneficial bacteria.
- **Consume Probiotics**- (contained in foods like yogurt, kimchi, and miso). Probiotics introduce beneficial bacteria to your gut.
- **Incorporate Prebiotics-** Prebiotic fibers feed the beneficial bacteria in your gut. (things like garlic, onions, bananas, asparagus)
- **Limit Processed Foods and Sugar-** Try to limit your consumption of things like artificial sweeteners and refined carbs.
- **Stay Hydrated-** Consuming enough water helps maintain the mucosal lining of the gut and also supports healthy digestion.

What you eat matters tremendously. The gut microbiome is central to your mental and physical health, affecting your digestion, immunity, and mood. I noticed more productivity, better brain functioning, more creativity, and an overall better outlook on life the moment I became more disciplined in eating better. Taking steps to protect and nourish your body leads to a higher quality of life. Being more aware of your body consumption is paramount, but so is nourishing your mind.

I also began to read regularly. And to be frank, I'm not talking about reading creepy mystery books or undying romance novels. I mean mindset books, self-love, business, and practically anything that could elevate my life and teach me how to cope. Some of the books I've read and enjoyed that assisted in my personal transformation include "Buy Yourself The Damn Flowers" by Tam Kaur, "The Four Agreements" by Miguel Ruiz, and one of my all-time favorites, "The Subtle Art of Not Giving A F*ck" by Mark Manson. All of these books place great emphasis on loving yourself, enhancing your self-concept, and altering the internal to experience the external transformation you desire. The absolute best and most significant book that I read was the word of God, the Bible; I became enlightened and more spiritually connected to God on a soul level. If you truly understand the Bible, you'll realize that each story became a testimony, showing you what a little bit of faith, obedience, and mindfulness can do.

"And be not conformed to this world: but be ye transformed by the renewing of your mind, that ye may prove what is that good, and acceptable, and perfect, will of God."
-Romans 12:2 (KJV)

I gained a deeper connection in my spirituality, intuition, and emotional intelligence. I learned how to truly utilize my spirit mind and my conscious mind. Some religious people refer to their spirit mind as the Holy Spirit. Meditation and mindfulness became my lifestyle. In the past I often allowed my racing thoughts to impact my moods daily. Now instead I practice being present, letting go of what happened before, and not being pressured into anxiety about the future, but just being present. I began grounding myself—walking barefoot in the grass, hugging trees, and spending a significant amount of time in sunlight and nature. Not only is this a way to enhance emotional intelligence and promote mindfulness, but it is also a way of nourishing your soul and increasing your intuition, that deep connection with your soul. Practice becoming fully submerged in the present moment. When I allowed 'grounding' to become a habit, I gained mental clarity. I became more inclined to make not only knowledge-based but 'soul-based' decisions, often referred to as practicing discernment. Spending time outdoors, whether walking in a forest, sitting by the ocean, or gazing at the stars, contributes to you feeling more connected to God. It gives you a better or 'higher' perspective on your place in the world. You'll cultivate a better understanding of your life's purpose, develop better emotional regulation, and enhance your self-concept. You'll also begin to foster deeper, more authentic connections with people.

Love, understanding, and mutual support are some of the highest forms of receiving external nourishment for your soul. Pair that with an overload of gratitude. No matter where you are in life or how bad you may think it is, you should always find something to be grateful for. When you think about things that make you feel happy, it instantly raises your frequency. You feel a vibration in your soul that instantly lifts your spirits, literally. This frequency will create your new bold and divine identity.

You must also commit to continuous learning and consistent mental stimulation. Become dedicated to nourishing your mind, and watch your mind expand. You'll start to think more 'outside the box,' past peers and societal pressures. Explore topics that expand your knowledge and inspire you. Don't be afraid to invest in things like courses, mentorships, and communities. Be willing to take it all the way and become abnormally obsessed with growth.

I eat, sleep, and breathe personal development. I constantly pour into myself and find ways to grow my mindset. My philosophy is it took me this long to 'wake up and smell the coffee,' so it may take me just as long to transform and transition fully into my new identity, my written divine destiny. That version of me already exists. It's just waiting patiently for me to actually become the version of me capable of handling my new identity. You must become disciplined, willing to do the work, and patient.

Dive deep into your creativity and expression. Journaling, creative writing, and storytelling allow you to process emotions and express your thoughts more freely. Dance in the rain. No, seriously, dance in the rain. Or just dance. Listening to or creating music and moving to it promotes emotional release and mental relaxation, nourishing your mind, creativity, and your soul. Most of the time, when you find yourself in a rut, if you listen to sad music, it seems to feed the sadness. You become sadder. Or at least you feel that way. If you listen to more happy, upbeat music, you'll find yourself singing, dancing, and in a better mood.

Most people don't talk about adequate mental rest. Prioritize sleep to cultivate better memory focus and emotional stability. Take breaks. Step away from work periodically to refresh your mind. Become lost in curiosity: try new things, learn a new language, cook a new dish. Engage in new and fresh activities that ignite joy from deep within. Engage in past times that ignite your inner radiant energy.

The energy you put out depends on the internal flow of energy. Chakras represent the flow of energy within your body, which directly connects to the universal flow of energy around you. Understanding chakras can help you focus more deeply on energy alignment and more balance. Chakras are all about achieving balance and harmony within yourself, both essential for nourishing all aspects of your being. There are 7 main chakras. Here's a breakdown of the seven chakras, their functions, and how they affect your life and energy.

#1) Root Chakra
- Location: Base of the Spine
- Color: Red
- Element: Earth
- Represents: Stability, security, grounding, and survival (basic needs like food, shelter, and safety).

When your root chakra is imbalanced, you may feel fear, anxiety, financial stability, or a disconnect from reality. When your root chakra is in its balanced state, you'll feel grounded, secure, and stable.

#2) Sacral Chakra
- Location: Lower abdomen, below the navel
- Color: Orange
- Element: Water
- Represents: Creativity, pleasure, emotions, sensuality, and relationships

When your Sacral Chakra is balanced, you may feel joyful, creative, and emotionally open. When your sacral chakra is imbalanced, you may feel disconnected, emotionally unstable, or blocked creatively.

#3) Solar Plexus Chakra

- Location: Upper abdomen, stomach area
- Color: Yellow
- Element: Fire
- Represents: Confidence, personal power, willpower, self-esteem

When your solar plexus chakra is imbalanced, you may feel powerless, lack confidence, or struggle with a lot of self-doubt. When your solar plexus chakra is balanced, you feel confident, self-assured, and motivated.

#4) Heart Chakra

- Location: Center of the chest
- Color: Green
- Element: Air
- Represents: Love, compassion, forgiveness, emotional balance

When your heart chakra is imbalanced, you may feel lonely, bitter, or unable to give/receive love. When your heart chakra is balanced, you'll feel love for yourself and others and cultivate healthy relationships.

#5) Throat Chakra

- Location: Throat
- Color: Blue
- Element: Ether (Space)
- Represents: Communication, truth, self-expression

When your throat chakra is imbalanced, you may feel silenced, misunderstood, or unable to speak your truth. When your throat chakra is balanced, you may feel more comfortable expressing yourself clearly and authentically.

#6) Third Eye Chakra

- Location: Between the eyebrows
- Color: Indigo
- Element: Light
- Represents: Intuition, insight, imagination, wisdom

When your third eye chakra is imbalanced, you may feel indecisive, disconnected, or lacking foresight. When your third eye chakra is balanced, you'll be more comfortable trusting your intuition and trusting yourself for clarity of thought.

#7) Crown Chakra

- Location: Top of head
- Color: Violet or White
- Element: Thought/Spirit
- Represents: Spiritual connection, enlightenment, higher consciousness

When your crown chakra is imbalanced, you might feel spiritually disconnected or struggle with meaning in life. When your crown chakra is balanced, you may feel connected to a higher power (God) and at peace.

Each chakra corresponds to specific aspects of your life, such as emotions, behaviors, and physical functions. They act as energy hubs, receiving and radiating energy throughout your body. When your chakras are balanced and open, energy flows freely, promoting harmony and well-being. If a chakra becomes blocked or imbalanced, it can lead to physical, emotional, and even spiritual challenges. Simply put, chakras represent the inner work you do to stay aligned and harmonious. Making them a powerful system for sustaining and nourishing your mind, body, and soul and helping you align with your highest potential. Addressing your chakra imbalances helps you release old wounds and limiting beliefs, clearing the way for healing, transformation, and growth. You also become more comfortable in your authenticity because each chakra contributes to understanding and expressing your true self, helping you embrace your identity fully.

Let me just be transparent: all three of my chakras were chaotically imbalanced, unaligned, and just plain old out of whack. My self-concept was completely gone. My stress levels were always abnormally high. I was living in scarcity, ripping and running the streets with no sense of stability. So, if you, like me, read through this list of chakras and realized that one, two, maybe even three of your chakras seem to be imbalanced, how do you go about becoming more balanced? Energy healing through methods like meditation and yoga works tremendously. Deep, intentional breathing (breathwork) clears energy channels. Living a balanced lifestyle also promotes rapid chakra health—a healthy diet, exercise, and sleep. Spending time in nature restores your energetic balance. Here are some more specific ways for you to embrace consistently balancing each chakra:

Balancing Your Root Chakra:

- Grounding Exercises: Walk barefoot on grass, sand, or soil to connect with the Earth.
- Affirmation: "I am safe, secure, and grounded."
- Consume red foods like beets, tomatoes, strawberries, and root vegetables like potatoes and carrots.
- Yoga Poses: Mountain pose, warrior pose, or tree pose.

Balancing Your Sacral Chakra:

- Engage in creativity: Paint, write, dance, or do something playful
- Affirmation: "I allow myself to feel joy and embrace my creativity."
- Consume orange foods like oranges, carrots, and sweet potatoes. (Water-rich foods)
- Yoga Poses: Cobra pose, butterfly pose, or hip openers

Balancing Your Solar Plexus Chakra:

- Set Goals: Take small, confident steps toward a personal goal

- Affirmation: "I am confident, beautiful and powerful. I am in control of my life."
- Consume yellow foods like bananas, corn, and lemons. Also, whole grains.
- Yoga Poses: Boat Pose, plank pose, or twists

Balancing Your Heart Chakra:

- Practice Gratitude: Keep a journal daily of the things you're thankful for.
- Affirmation: "I give and receive love freely and unconditionally."
- Consume green foods like spinach, broccoli, and kale. Drink herbal teas.
- Yoga Poses: Camel pose, cobra pose, or heart openers

Balancing Your Throat Chakra:

- Speak Your Truth: Practice sharing thoughts authentically, even in small ways.
- Affirmation: "I speak clearly, confidently, and with purpose."
- Consume blue foods like blueberries and blackberries. Drink herbal teas.
- Yoga Poses: Fish pose, shoulder stand, or neck stretches.

Balancing Your Third Eye Chakra:

- Meditate: Focus on your forehead and visualize an indigo light.

- Affirmation: "I wholeheartedly trust my intuition and inner wisdom."
- Consime purple foods like grapes, eggplant, and purple cabbage. Consume dark chocolate.
- Yoga Poses: Child's pose, downward dog, or eagle pose.

Balancing Your Crown Chakra:

- Meditation: Focus on the top of your head and visualize white or violet light.
- Affirmation: "I am connected to my divine God-given energy and wisdom."
- Consume light foods like herbal teas, water, and fruits.
- Yoga Poses: Headstand, lotus pose, or corpse pose.

Intentionally being aware of your chakras and their state is a sure way to enhance your overall state of mind and well-being. Be very mindful of how you spend your time. Commit to consistently practicing meditation, citing affirmations, yoga, and rewiring your mind for abundance. Your new identity requires you to become new, brand-spanking new. Be mindful of what you choose to consume, and remain committed to eating food that supports each chakra and your overall well-being. Regularly check in with yourself and identify and release negative emotions. Consistently incorporate prayer, gratitude, and quiet reflection in your daily habits. Remain aware of your inner energy and how energy is being transferred to you. Deepen your connection with God, and become more in tune spiritually. Enhance your discernment. From this moment forward, make a vow to embrace your body, mind, and soul as a temple. Nourish and protect them like your life depends on it, well, because it quite literally does.

Dear Me,

I see you. I truly see you—the real you buried underneath. I love you and value you right where you are. I acknowledge how much you've grown, how much you've endured, and how deeply you desire to live a life that feels whole and fulfilling. This is a gentle reminder to me to care for myself not just in passing but intentionally, deeply, and unapologetically. I vow to feed you only thoughts that elevate you and cultivate an environment for growth. I will protect you fiercely by being more mindful of what I consume. Not just in regard to food but when it comes to books, media, and conversations. I understand that these factors affect how I see the world and myself. I will fill my mind only with truths that empower me and remind me of who I am and what I am capable of. I deserve to believe in my brilliance. I vow to feed my body with love and care, not only in what I choose to consume with my mouth but with how I move, rest, and speak to myself. My body is my home and constant companion and has carried me through every joy, heartbreak, and challenge. I understand now that my body only asks me for kindness in return. I vow to feed my soul with things that set it on fire. I unapologetically embrace quiet moments of stillness and isolation and only align with connections that feel like home. I see the beauty in small things like the warmth of the sunlight on my skin, the sound of rain, and the comfort of a soft breeze. I understand that my soul thrives in the simple moments, in the spaces where love and peace reside. I know now that I can no longer pour from an empty cup, nor can I thrive on fragments. I vow to give myself the care and nourishment that I so willingly give to others. I am ready to feel whole again, and this is a commitment to myself to choose me every single day!

With endless love and gratitude,

ME

CHAPTER 5:

Illuminating The Mirror
Harnessing Your Inner Energy

∞

Now, this may sound crazy to you, especially if you're religious and identify as a 'Christian,' but open your mind and hear me out. In my last few years on this journey, I've researched and learned a lot. I've become extremely open-minded and spiritually connected. I don't consider myself religious; I am spiritual and divinely connected to God. I do believe in the trinity and that Jesus died on the cross for our sins. I've also educated myself about the laws of the universe—laws like the law of attraction, the law of detachment, and the concept of manifestation. I regard these as spiritual laws. Please hear me out. I firmly believe in God being above all and the creator of the universe, but I also believe these laws and principles are very significant in becoming your highest self and transforming your identity. I regard these 'laws' as pivotal spiritual practices in releasing the strongholds of worldly captivity that were intentionally placed upon you.

These could explain those unwarranted feelings like thinking you aren't enough, the constant need to be perfect or accepted, and the feeling that abundance is hard and not your birthright. Earlier, we talked about the subconscious mind and the role it plays in obtaining the life you envision. The issue is once we experience trauma, it becomes planted in our subconscious mind, then creates an automatic implanted reaction. Identical to experiencing struggle or scarcity. Stay with me. You only need to experience or become traumatized by something one time for it to become a belief. For example, if you've ever been cheated on, you probably carry the belief that all men are dishonest. You might struggle with prevalent trust issues and insecurities. Despite your new partner being nothing like the last, that belief will still stand until your subconscious can consistently be proven wrong and becomes rewired to a new belief.

In the past, I've had a negative correlation between relationships and social media. I've consistently seen too much disloyalty in the way men choose to navigate or 'move' on social media. Therefore, I developed the belief that men who use social media are problematic, dishonest, and disloyal. Without them doing anything wrong, I become accusatory by nature. In my own shadow work, identifying my triggers, and becoming more self-aware, I was able to rewire these subconscious beliefs. The same concept applies to scarcity and your mindset around success. How you think creates an emotion, and that emotion creates a feeling, and that feeling becomes a belief. That belief can trigger 'inspired action' or lack thereof. Your lack of willingness to try means you have no results. When you have no results, you create false anxiety, depression, comparison, self-doubt, fear, etc. Once you have unbelief, it's hard to also have true, unwavering faith in something. No faith means staying where you are, trapped in the same belief system, and consequently, trapped in the same life with absolutely no movement. You'll find yourself stuck doing the same things over and over and breeding the same results each time. I don't care how much you say you believe in God and his word; it's impossible for you to truly believe wholeheartedly without faith.

The 'inspired action' is the works mentioned in the very popular bible verse, "Faith without works is dead," derived from the book of James. Understand that God is the source of all power, not the universe, but you have to really believe in God, not just the idea. You must truly have faith that all things are working out in your favor. This could be why you've been praying and praying and have become weary because nothing is shifting in your reality. Manifestation says that in order for anything to 'shift' in your reality, you must first truly believe energetically. Just like with prayer, in order to believe, you have to know without a doubt that God exists and His word is true. How can you truly believe if you don't believe?!

I believe that in order for you to shift from scarcity back to abundance, you must first re-wire your mind and re-align with the wholeness of God's creation, the universe, as well as the spiritual laws of the universe. You must undo the damage that was created by your external realities and understand the power you have within. Understand that abundance is and always has been your birthright. The world just does a good job of tricking you out of your spot. They know that once you truly lose your faith, there will be no action. You are much more valuable to them as an insecure, powerless consumer. They intentionally shake up your God-given beliefs and cause you to succumb to the ways, thoughts, and belief systems of the world. You must build, cultivate, and thrive from a different frequency in order for 'faith' to work. Here's how it all connects when it comes to the spiritual concept of manifestation:

1. Faith activates the process.
2. Prayer and intention set the vision.
3. Gratitude keeps your heart aligned with God's abundance.
4. Action and obedience show your commitment.
5. Trust in God ensures that the outcome is aligned with His plan for your highest good.

Manifestation, at its highest purpose, is an act of faith in God's power, promises, and timing. I like to say a re-activation. You will feel this activation; it will show in your frequency. Some call it a spiritual breakthrough. When you can no longer 'vibrate' or feel on this spiritual frequency, you will never truly trust, believe, or "walk by faith and not by sight." You probably won't walk [take significant (inspired) action to claim your abundance] at all. Manifestation truly demonstrates the power of faith and gives you actionable steps in rebuilding your spiritual mind and abundant belief system when it has been lost, buried, or stolen! It requires you to believe in the unseen through affirmations that reaffirm your belief in abundance. You can utilize visualization to see where God is calling you to be and what your purpose is, as well as to cultivate an energy of gratitude. The more you affirm, the more you erase the learned beliefs and create new beliefs. The more you visualize, the more you see, so the more you believe. The more you're able to feel and remember that high frequency, the more eventually it'll become the default. The Holy Spirit will be re-instated. The feelings of scarcity will disappear, and the low frequency or doubt will surface less and less. The Bible says,

"Now faith is the substance of things hoped for, the evidence of things not seen." -**Hebrews 11:1 (KJV)**

When you allow yourself to see and believe in your purpose, you become more willing to step out in faith. When you step out in faith, affirming and working toward something that hasn't yet materialized, you're practicing a core biblical principle. As you see these 'manifestations' or God's promises come to fruition, your faith in God's power to change your situation grows more and more. You experience firsthand how genuine, untainted belief activates God's blessing. When you manifest and visualize with God in your heart as your guide, you naturally seek His input on your desires, suppressing the negative subconscious belief system and believing wholeheartedly in His will. You create a deeper sense of purpose and trust in His plan. As you see how His path for you unfolds (which in most cases leads to the 'inspired action'), you come to trust Him more naturally and wholeheartedly. Essentially, you are co-creating with God. You set the intentions, take the action, and trust Him to handle the rest.

In no way, shape, or form is manifestation intended to replace God or relying solely on yourself. It's about deepening your partnership with Him through unwavering faith. After all, how many times have you actually seen things happen without you stepping out in faith? Whether it be introducing yourself to that person or moving to that new city, all of God's plans for your life will require some sort of action from you to be carried out. How can you take action if you have been trained to sit, wait, and sulk instead of believe, have faith, and receive? Each manifestation that aligns with God's will becomes a tangible reminder of His endless love, power, and faithfulness. As you see His promises fulfilled in your life, your faith grows stronger, inspiring you to take action more quickly and have a more sure mindset. Your belief in God's goodness becomes unshakeable. Your faith grows. Think of it like this: On the one hand, you're empowering yourself. On the other hand, you're empowering and deepening your connection with God. Both are prerequisites for stepping into your new identity.

The laws of the universe are spiritual principles that describe how energy, thought, and action shape the natural, living world and our experiences within it. These spiritual laws govern spirituality in the 'real world' or your reality but are derived from the spiritual world. In total, there are 12 laws. A lot of Christians or religious people decline to trust in these laws. However, I feel they are significant in developing true and unwavering faith. I believe the source should ALWAYS be recognized as God, but these spiritual laws govern both the physical and spiritual aspects of life. They create divine order that helps you to navigate and influence your human experience. I truly believe these laws were created to help those who experienced trauma and were formerly conforming to the ways of the world. They help you re-align with your higher consciousness, divine order, and inner peace.

> *"For by him were all things created, that are in heaven, and that are in Earth, visible and invisible, whether they be by thrones, or dominions, or principalities, or powers; all things were created by him, and for him:"* **-Colossians 1:16 (KJV)**

Here are what I consider to be the 12 spiritual laws of the universe and their relation to God's word:

The Law of Divine Oneness

- **Core Idea:** Everything in the universe is connected. Every thought, action, and event is intertwined, influencing the collective whole.

- **Practical Meaning**: Your actions and thoughts impact not only your life but also others around you. This law emphasizes the importance of compassion, unity, and understanding.

Biblical Parallel:

> *"For by him were all things created, that are in heaven, and that are in Earth, visible and invisible, whether they be thrones, or dominions, or principalities, or powers: all things were created by him, and for him: And he is before all things, and by him all things consist."*-**Colossians 1:16-17 (KJV)**

"All things were created by him and for him." This portion of the verse emphasizes that everything, seen and unseen, originates from a single divine source. That source is the creator, God. The law of divine oneness teaches that all creation is interconnected and part of a greater whole. "He is before all things" speaks again to God being the ultimate origin and source of all existence. The law of divine oneness reflects the idea that all things are part of one divine essence or consciousness. The last part of this verse reads, "By him all things consist." This confirms that everything in creation is held together by the divine force of God. Spiritually, this aligns with the belief that everything in the universe is connected, constantly influencing each other through this unseen divine essence.

The Law of Vibration

- **Core Idea**: Everything is energy and vibrates at its own frequency. Your thoughts and emotions emit vibrations that attract similar energies,
- **Practical Meaning**: Positive thoughts and feelings raise your vibration, attracting positive experiences. Negative energy does the same.

Biblical Parallel:

> *"Death and life are in the power of the tongue: and they that love it shall eat the fruit thereof."* -**Proverbs 18:21 (KJV)**

This verse illustrates that our words, which are vibrational energies, have the power to create or destroy. The law of vibration teaches that the frequencies we emit through our thoughts and speech influence the reality we experience. The law of vibration encourages you to maintain high-frequency thoughts, words, and actions. Spiritually, for me, this means that the vibrations from your words can uplift, heal, and inspire (life) or harm, curse, and destroy (death). You choose what you speak. That's why it's so important to be mindful of your thoughts and words; they ultimately become your vibration and your life.

The Law of Attraction

- **Core Idea**: Like attracts like. You draw into your life whatever you focus on, whether positive or negative.

- **Practical Meaning**: By focusing on your desires with belief and action, you can manifest your goals. Conversely, dwelling on fear or negativity can attract unwanted outcomes.

Biblical Parallel:

> "*Therefore I say unto you, what things soever ye desire, when ye pray, believe that ye receive them, and ye shall have them.*"-**Mark 11:24 (KJV)**
>
> "*Thou shalt also decree a thing, and it shall be established unto thee: And the light shall shine upon thy ways.*"
>
> **-Job 22:28 (KJV)**

These passages directly align with the principle of manifestation through belief. They reiterate the idea that to receive something, you must first believe it is already yours. Believe you have it before you are physically able to see it. Faith and belief are the 'vibrational match' required to manifest or bring your desires to reality. You must pray with faith. Therefore, without faith, how can you bring your desired reality into manifestation? This law is very important and one of the most referred to when talking about laws of the universe. Not only is what you say out loud important and significant in what you 'attract' or shift into reality, but your inner thoughts are extremely important as well. That's why the internal work is so important. You can fool yourself and other people externally, but you can't trick your inner thoughts into a manifested reality. You must first really think and truly believe in your capability to receive abundance from God.

> *"For as he thinketh in his heart, so is he."*
> **-Proverbs 23:7 (KJV)**

This verse again supports the premise that if you don't truly believe in something in your heart, you won't be able to receive it. Your inner thoughts, beliefs, and feelings shape your reality. These components literally control your outer reality. Many people claim to stand behind and mirror the mindset, ideas, and lifestyles using the guidance in the Bible, but do they really? Why do we have such heavy belief in the external but such insignificant belief in the power of the internal, the power and belief in our self? It is not a sin to believe that you must have empowered yourself in order to align with God's promises. I actually believe more Christians would be successful and live in abundance if they added these very principles that are also present in their Bibles to their daily lives. With this secret weapon, you'll be able to rebuild, rewire, and truly attract more of God's promises. If we can collectively be more open-minded to embracing truth based on subjective facts, we'd all be in a better place. Once I stopped trying to find information to support my current belief system and actually focused on actual subjective facts, data, and research, I was able to add significant actionable steps to my daily routine that helped me re-ignite my faith in God and become truly aligned with the new life I desired.

The Law of Correspondence

- **Core Idea**: As above, so below; as within, so without. Your outer world is a reflection of your inner world.
- **Practical Meaning**: To create a positive change in your external life, you must first change your mindset, beliefs, and emotional state.

Biblical Parallel: Now, for this biblical parallel, you can use the same verse and premise from the law of attraction, which is:

> *"For as he thinketh in his heart, so is he."*
>
> **-Proverbs 23:7 (KJV)**

But another verse that resonates with me when I think about the Law of Correspondence is derived from the book of Matthew:

> *"A good man out of the good treasure of the heart bringeth forth good things: and an evil man out of evil treasure bringeth forth evil things."-**Matthew 12:35 (KJV)***

Your inner world (your heart posture) directly corresponds to your outer actions and experiences. A "good treasure" in the heart produces good results (manifestations) in life, while an "evil treasure" results in negative outcomes. The heart is a storehouse of treasure. The mind is a storehouse of your personal thoughts and beliefs that were derived from your experiences or, as mentioned earlier, external influences: your parents, peers, mass media, etc. These storehouses directly influence what we "bring forth" or manifest in our lives. If everything was solely based on 'trusting' the word of God, how would these scriptures be valid? They clearly display God's expectations in regard to receiving the things you pray for. Numerous times, He emphasizes the importance of belief and having faith. In Florence Scove Shinn's book "The Game of Life and How to Play It," she talks about this very concept. "As within so without." She speaks about how the enlightened man strives to perfect himself, like Jesus. She goes on to say that a man's enemies are within himself, and the work that needs to be done is within—no anxiety, no depression, just good energy and thriving for perfection, gratitude, and grace.

The Law of Cause & Effect

- **Core Idea**: Every action has an equal and opposite reaction. What you put out into the world returns to you.
- **Practical Meaning**: Your choices and actions create a ripple effect, so act with intention and responsibility.

Biblical Parallel:

> "Be not deceived; God is not mocked: for whatsoever a man soweth, that shall he also reap."-**Galatians 6:7 (KJV)**

I'm sure you've probably heard this verse before, as it is very popular. This verse teaches that every seed (cause) we plant—through actions, thoughts, and behaviors—will result in a harvest (effect). Therefore, when we sow goodness, kindness, righteousness, and positivity, we will reap blessings and prosperity. When we sow sin, negativity, and wickedness, we will reap destruction and hardship. In short, what you put out into the world will return to you. If you allow yourself to succumb to scarcity, negativity, and low self-worth, well, that could certainly be why you're praying or manifesting and continuing to yield no results. This is why I express the importance of being self-aware and healing internally in order to shift your mindset and transform your life.

The Law of Compensation

- **Core Idea**: Rewards or consequences come from your efforts, actions, and contributions.
- **Practical Meaning**: Hard work, generosity, and kindness are eventually rewarded, even if not immediately visible.

Biblical Parallel:

> *"But this I say, He which soweth sparingly shall reap also sparingly; and he which soweth bountifully shall reap also bountifully."-2 Corinthians 9:6 (KJV)*

The more you give, whether it be in effort, time, or resources, the more you will receive in return. If you give little, you will receive little; If you're able and you give generously, you will receive abundantly.

Another verse that really drives this principle home can be found in Colossians:

*"And whatsoever ye do, do it heartily, as to the Lord, and not unto men; knowing that of the Lord ye shall receive the reward of the inheritance: for ye serve the Lord Christ."-**Colossians 3:23-24 (KJV)***

I love this verse because it highlights the principle that serving others not only brings blessings from them in return but also ensures that God will bless you for your service. When you work diligently, not just for human recognition but as a service to God, you will receive a divine reward. This verse also introduces the idea that compensation may not always be financial or material; it can also be in spiritual rewards, inheritance, and blessings from God. Good work, faithfulness, and excellence will always be rewarded. The source of the compensation is God and is even greater than human rewards.

The Law of Perpetual Transmutation of Energy

- **Core Idea**: Energy is constantly in motion and can be transformed. High vibrational energy can transform low vibrational energy.
- **Practical Meaning**: You have the power to change your circumstances by shifting your energy and thoughts to a higher frequency.

Biblical Parallel:

*"To every thing there is a season and a time to every purpose under the heaven"-**Ecclesiastes 3:1 (KJV)***

This emphasizes the cycles of change under the heaven, which can be seen as reality, the living world, or the 'universe.' Nothing remains the same. The perpetual movement of time and the shift in seasons show how life (your human experience/natural reality) is in a constant state of change. No condition is permanent, and the essence of life is always flowing into a new form.

The Law of Relativity

- **Core Idea**: Everything is relative; the challenges, situations, or blessings in life are only significant when compared to something else.
- **Practical Meaning**: This law emphasizes perspective, gratitude, and reliance on God. Basically, your perspective creates your reality. Your perspective guides your comparison.

Biblical Parallel:

"For our light affliction, which is but for a moment, worketh for us a far more exceeding and external weight of glory; While we look not at the things which are seen, but at the things which are not seen: for the things which are seen are temporal; but the things which are not seen are eternal." -2 Corinthians 4:17-18 (KJV)

This verse places earthly struggles in perspective by comparing them to the eternal glory of God's promises, showing that life's challenges are relative when viewed in the light of eternity. If you live by this premise, again, your perspective changes drastically.

The Law of Polarity

- **Core Idea:** Everything has an opposite: light/dark, good/bad, hot/cold. Opposites are necessary for balance and understanding.
- **Practical Meaning:** Everything has an opposite, and these opposites are inherently connected. Without one, the other could not exist, as the contrast between the two is what gives them meaning. Difficult times help you appreciate the good. Understanding polarity helps you find balance in life.

Biblical Parallel:

> *"I form the light, and create darkness: I make peace, and create evil: I the Lord do all these things."-Isaiah 45:7 (KJV)*

This verse acknowledges that God created both light and darkness, showing that opposites are part of the balance of creation. Never expect one without the other being present as well. Life's dualities are essential for growth and better understanding. When we embrace this truth, we can navigate life with more resilience, gratitude, and hope.

The Law of Rhythm

- **Core Idea**: Life operates in cycles, like the seasons or tides. Everything flows in natural rhythms.

- **Practical Meaning**: Life is always in motion, and this motion creates ebb and flow, much like the tides of the ocean. This law is a reminder to trust the natural flow of life, understanding that highs and lows are part of the same rhythm.

Biblical Parallel:

> *"To every thing there is a season, and a time to every purpose under the heaven: A time to be born, and a time to die; a time to plant, and a time to pluck up that which is planted." -Ecclesiastes 3:1-8 (KJV)*

This verse beautifully reflects life's rhythms and the necessity of each phase. We are reminded to trust the process, embrace change, and find peace in the inevitability of cycles. It teaches that even in life's storms, calm waters will follow.

The Law of Gender

- **Core Idea**: Everything has masculine (action-oriented) and feminine (receptive, nurturing) energy.
- **Practical Meaning**: Each of these energies are present in all people and throughout nature. It's important to balance these energies within yourself to achieve harmony. For example, pair action with intuition or drive with patience.

Biblical Parallel:

> *"So God created man in his own image, in the image of God created he him; male and female created he them."-*
> ***Genesis 1:27 (KJV)***

This verse highlights the duality of masculine and feminine in God's creation. Harmony and balance between these energies are key to fulfillment. Recognizing and aligning these energies can lead to a more productive, peaceful, and creative life.

The Law of Unity/Divine Purpose

- **Core Idea**: All things in the universe are interconnected and part of a greater divine plan.
- **Practical Meaning**: Everything happens for a reason, guided by a higher purpose, and that we are all connected through God's divine will. Trust that your life has meaning and that every experience, whether joyful or challenging, contributes to your growth and spiritual evolution.

Biblical Parallel:

> *"And we know that all things work together for good to them that love God, to them who are the called according to his purpose." -**Romans 8:28 (KJV)***

This verse highlights the unity of all believers under one God, reflecting divine oneness. You need to see yourself as a greater whole, guided by God's love and plan. By embracing unity, love, and service, we align with our divine purpose and contribute to the harmony of creation.

These principles govern how energy and intention shape our spiritual reality. We've talked about shadow work previously, which, too, contributes tremendously to ridding yourself of scarcity and being able to recognize the abundant things that

God blessed us with. You can't truly walk by faith if you've experienced so much trauma that it stifles you subconsciously. You start to surface-level believe and do not truly have the spiritual connection of belief, the soul-level of belief. I don't care how much you claim you believe in God and claim to have faith; if your inner energy doesn't truly reflect that belief, you'll never be able to see the glass as half full. Your heart posture must be pure and untainted.

These spiritual principles align closely with the same spiritual truths found in the Bible, proving that divine wisdom and universal order are deeply interconnected. God should be the only one in the equation who should be worshipped, not the universe, nor should these laws. These principles are merely stepping stones and actionable tools for the internal transformation required to walk in your spiritual enlightenment. When we sow love, kindness, and faith, we reap blessings and abundance. Basically, what we put out, we receive back. In essence, the laws of the universe, or spiritual laws, are reflections of God's divine order. They work because they are rooted in spiritual truths established by the creator, God. When you think of manifestation, the laws of the universe, and other principles, you realize they are solely to build your faith and belief system, which consequently will build your spirituality and connection to God. This perspective bridges the gap between spirituality and practical universal principles, illustrating that they are not separate but, in fact, deeply intertwined. Each portion empowers its necessary counterpart, creating a healthier, more abundant frequency and aiding tremendously in your personal self-development and shifting your reality.

Dear Me,

I see the woman you're committed to becoming—wise, powerful, and fully aligned with divine order, ready and willing to walk in your purpose and fulfill your assignment. I've spent so much time searching for clarity, not realizing that the answers were already written within me and my sacred book of truth, the Bible. I will constantly remind myself that I am a reflection of God's creative power. I now understand that even though God promised me abundance, work will also required from me to bring me full circle into my destiny and new identity. I understand that spiritual laws aren't separate from God but interconnected and rooted in Him. I am a co-creator with God. I understand that every thought, every word, and every action I release into the world is a seed. I commit to only speaking life into myself because I know that I will reap what I sew. I will move with intention and refuse to shrink myself. I will no longer limit my desires out of fear of "doing too much." God didn't create me to be content with doing "just enough"; he called me to do exceedingly and abundantly above all I can ask or think. His only requirement is that I vow to meet him halfway. I will speak boldly and confidently. Say it, see it, believe it. I will take responsibility for my seeds. I understand that if I want a better harvest, I should plant better seeds. Today, I will no longer find comfort in fleeing the desires God has planted in my heart. My dreams are never too big, and my vision is never too much. My vision is divine, and from this point forward, I vow to own it and truly walk in the light God placed within me. In my daily endeavors, I am encouraged to remind myself that the same God who created this universe also placed his spirit within me.

With Love & Power,

Me

CHAPTER 6

The Mirror Speaks

Words that Shape Your Reflection

∞

"Death and life are in the power of the tongue:
and they that love it shall eat the fruit thereof."
-Proverbs 18:21 (KJV)

This scripture highlights that our words hold immense creative power. When we speak positive, faith-filled statements, we align with God's promises and the universal truth that our words shape our reality. Speaking life into our circumstances through affirmations mirrors how 'the tongue' alone can alter our belief system and alter our lives for the better. This is very significant in self-development. Affirmations are positive, faith-filled statements spoken aloud or internally to reinforce belief, shift mindsets, and shape reality. While the modern concept of affirmations is popular in personal development and self-help, the idea of speaking words of life, faith, and power has deep biblical roots. The Bible repeatedly emphasizes the power of words, declarations, and confessions of faith. The words we speak produce "fruit" (results) in our lives. If you continuously speak negativity, doubt, and fear, you eat the fruit of destruction, therefore producing that very fruit.

Affirmations are "I am" statements that allow you to reclaim and align with your power. "I am" statements changed my life. Constantly rewiring my thoughts and statements allowed my subconscious to believe these statements and who I am. I had to completely erase my old thought pattern as it only aligned with the thoughts and beliefs of "I used to be," not who I aspired to become. It is imperative that you do the same not only when your mind is in beta but, more importantly, when you start to experience those negative spiraling thoughts and emotions. Your emotions have to connect with NEW thoughts to create a new belief system. This new belief system creates your new life—the life that aligns with your identity in God.

When your mind is in the beta brainwave state, it means your brain is operating at a high-frequency level of activity. Beta is when your conscious thinking, problem-solving, logic, and alert brain waves are active. In the beta state, your conscious mind is active. This allows you to actively choose and direct your thoughts. Beta is best for creating conscious shifts. Your focus and attention are at their peak. You have conscious control over your thoughts. When your mind is in beta, it's a lot easier to reframe those negative thoughts as they come and actually retain the new pattern of thinking. If you affirm, "I am worthy, valuable, and irreplaceable just as I am," and your mind says, "No, you're not," you can counter with logic like, "My past does not define me. God's word says I am fearfully and wonderfully made. I am worthy, and nothing can separate me from God's love." After doing this consciously and daily, I began to notice that my thoughts had actually shifted. My mind started to believe what I was saying. I started to glow more and feel more confident, and my life started to reflect that inner confidence externally.

In the Bible, God himself identifies as "I am." We, as believers, are called to align our identity with God's truth. In Genesis, God talks about creating us in His very likeness. This is why, throughout this text, I've expressed the importance of taking actionable steps to rebuild your self-confidence and know who you are. Rebuilding is literally the most significant and impactful part of your journey. You will not identify with your new, higher identity unless you completely rid yourself of the old identity—the old thought patterns, emotions, and beliefs.

"Let the weak say, I am strong."-Joel 3:10 (KJV)

This verse encourages us to speak strength into our lives and declare the opposite of what we feel in the natural. Therefore, if you feel weak, you must still declare or *affirm* strength; even if you feel defeated, you must declare victory. This same concept applies when rebuilding your self-concept. When I felt broken, unworthy, and ugly, I would affirm that

I was brave, worthy, and beautiful instead, regardless of what I actually thought. Eventually, I started to believe it, and the people around me did too. I started to hear compliments like, "You are glowing" and "You have good energy." Even now, I constantly get compliments from strangers, whether it be about my looks, my clothing, or my aura. The aura compliments are my favorite ones. To date, I still have never stopped affirming who I am. I constantly compliment myself and tell myself I am worthy. Just like the saying, "Talk to Me Nice," you have to speak to yourself nicely. Watch how you not only start to feel that way, but it'll also begin to shine through in your outer appearance. At this very moment, it's very important for you to understand that your words are not casual. They are forces of power. Forces of power that can alter your entire life for the better. Be intentional. Be consistent. Feel it in your heart and soul as you recite. Here are some Biblically based self-concept building affirmations:

> "I am fearfully and wonderfully made."
> "I am worthy, valuable, and irreplaceable just as I am."
> "I am confident in every room I walk into because I walk with God."
> "I am walking in my purpose, and God placed everything I need within me."

Create your own "I am" affirmations based on the things you struggle with in your own personal journey. Remember, you are everything God says you are. Not only are you a product of Him, but He placed himself inside of you; therefore, you have God's power within. Please understand that this world is dedicated to doing everything in its power to help you forget who you are so they can instead capitalize off your insecurities and weaknesses. The other half of the natural world, the religious world, wants you to believe that everything you need is with God and the bible, which is very true, but they forget to remind you of the imminent power you hold within. This is your reminder that everything you need is within, and you lack nothing. You are indeed your very own secret weapon.

Dear Me,

Now's the time to make the shift into my divine power. Take a look at yourself, truly look—not just at the surface but at the soul behind the eyes staring back at me. I know now that my words have power, more power than I've acknowledged in the past. I want to first apologize to myself for allowing my words to bring me down instead of using them as a reminder of how powerful, bold, and beautiful I am. Every word I say shapes the way I think and act and who I decide to become. Affirmations are more than just positive thinking; they are declarations from me to me that challenge the inner doubt, fear, and insecurity I've held onto for far too long. Every day, my mind is listening, and every word I say to myself is like a seed being planted in the garden of my heart. I understand that when I speak life, faith, and love into myself, I grow stronger, more resilient, and deeply rooted in my self-worth. I know that the opposite is also true. I vow to remove words that bring fear, doubt, and criticism to the surface. I will no longer allow weeds of insecurity to take over. I understand that my commitment to reciting affirmations that uplift me daily will transform me greatly and shift me into my new identity: my dream version of myself. When I say "I am worthy" or "I am capable," I am fixing my heart and mind to truly believe in me. My words become thoughts, and those thoughts become actions. Those actions have the ability to shift my reality. I will no longer wait for others to affirm to me what God has already established. In my loudest, most loving voice, I now see how greatly "I am loved," "I am deserving of success and peace," and "I have everything I need to fulfill my purpose." I declare these to be true with confidence. I am committed to affirming them until they become second nature. I understand that the world will be relentless in trying to tell me who I am, but I have the authority to declare only who God says I am. I will use my tongue only to SPEAK LIFE. I will be kind, patient, and persistent with my words. I will give myself grace in understanding that it takes time to undo years of self-doubt, but every time I speak life into myself, I am rewriting my story. So, dear me, this is a reminder to speak life, love, and power. I am becoming everything God called me to be, unapologetically.

With love and unwavering belief,
ME

CHAPTER 7:

Your Sacred Reflection
Building Unshakeable Self-Worth

∞

The term sacred, by definition, refers to something that is regarded with reverence, holiness, or deep respect. Your perception of your own self-worth is parallel to the abundance you attract and the relationships you curate. Your self-worth is sacred. Building your self-worth taps into the divine essence within you, your light, the frequency you ignite, how you shine, and, ultimately, how you show up for yourself. At its core, self-worth is all about recognizing your inherent value, and that recognition is a deeply spiritual act. As your self-worth enhances, so will your self-concept. You hold a divine spark within you—a God-like illumination.

> *"So God created man in his own image, in the image of God created he him; male and female created he them."*
>   *-Genesis 1:27 (KJV)*

This verse goes on to talk about how we have been given dominion over everything. Most people who claim to believe in God have heard this verse a thousand times. Yet, most of them still don't believe in their own capability or self-worth. This goes along with what I mentioned earlier about being unable to truly believe unless you authentically believe. If you have zero faith in yourself, what energy do you have to believe in anything external? Your self-worth is a light that starts on the inside and can be seen by others on the outside. This is your divinity, your gift, your contribution to the world. When you affirm your worth with a powerful belief, you align with your higher self, step out of doubt, and step into divine consciousness. Many of your current beliefs about yourself are rooted in trauma, your conditioning from your peers/society, and past experiences. Releasing these beliefs for good is a sacred act of purification and a significant part of your blueprint for achieving true divine belief in one's power. When you love yourself, you are able to see yourself as a reflection of God. Love is the highest vibrational frequency. Embracing self-love is an act of returning to wholeness, allowing you to follow and trust your intuition. In this season, you will no longer need or crave external validation and can truly see yourself as worthy. You step out of "playing small" and fully embody your divine assignment on this Earth. Your purpose is divine, necessary, and, most importantly, sacred. It is a calling from your higher self. In this season, it's so important that you protect your inner-g or 'energy,' but mostly your inner-g (your inner God and your inner 'gangsta.') Gangsta in this context is your authenticity, intuition, and divine energy. Understand that every day is for harvesting when it pertains to the masses. Disconnected people will constantly try to 'harvest' or redirect your energy. The more of your energy you put into negativity, the less you have to re-ignite yourself. Boundaries are a sacred act of self-protection and will naturally elevate your self-worth and concept. You will cultivate a deeper connection with God and an enhancement of your 'discernment' or your ability to identify things that are sent to deter you. Boundaries are your spiritual armor. They ensure that your energy remains pure. Self-awareness, self-acceptance, and self-worth all work simultaneously in your favor, perfectly aligning you with your higher destiny and your higher self.

Sacred Affirmations to Build Self-Worth

- "I am a reflection of divine love and light."
- "My worth is not negotiable-it is sacred, whole, and eternal."
- "I am worthy of abundance, peace, and unconditional love."
- "I honor the divine in me by loving myself completely."
- "Every day, I remember that I am worthy of my dreams and desires."

To see yourself as worthy is to receive yourself as divine, whole, and sacred. You'll live life with more joy, peace, and authenticity. Commit to harnessing your self-worth and reclaim your rightful place as a co-creator of your reality. You are not here to 'earn' your worth. You are here to harness it, re-ignite the power within, and fulfill your purpose while re-igniting the light in others. When you decide to become a light for others, you inspire them to walk their sacred path, too. Not to mention, you cultivate a life truly worth living. You begin to embrace daily gratitude and an authentic heart grounded in peace, compassion, and unconditional love. Your prosperity is hidden in plain sight: within. The entire theme of this book has been rebooting your inner world to align with the promises of God, your purpose, and your destiny. With the newly gained internal validation, you can ignite external radiation with God as the source.

CHAPTER 8

The Radiant Magnetic Reflection

Becoming Her

∞

Now is the time to embrace your sacred reboot and let it shine outwardly. Go public and make an impact. No more self-doubt, chaos, confusion, or double-mindedness. No more seeking the world's acceptance. You have become radiant and undeniably confident. Your purpose is always at the forefront of your intentions, and your testimony aligns perfectly with your ultimate destiny. You are becoming healed, whole, deeply connected, and guided by God, in harmony with the universe. You are becoming HER.

What you see in the mirror has everything to do with how you perceive yourself internally. Your self-view is your self-concept. This is also the lens through which you'll choose to view the outer world and your actual physical reflection. Your thoughts, perceptions, and beliefs about your abilities, identity, worth, and purpose. Your self-concept shapes every aspect of your life—your confidence, the decisions you make, the goals you pursue, and even how you allow others to treat you. When your self-concept is strong, you will see yourself as worthy, capable, deserving, and beautiful. If your self-concept is weak or negative, you might feel inadequate, unworthy, or powerless. Essentially, it's all about the way you define yourself, the picture you hold in your mind about yourself. Utilizing every tool in this text will not only enhance your self-concept but teach other people how to treat you and allow you to reset your standards, move with excellence, and steal your power back.

You should also include mirror work in your daily regimen and commit to it. Look yourself in the eyes with your full presence and see yourself through the lens of unconditional love. Focus solely on your positive attributes externally and internally. When you view yourself daily with love and not judgment, you shift your internal narrative. Your mindset shifts from "I'm not enough" to "I see myself clearly, and I am enough." The time has come for you to break down the illusions of inadequacy and shift the internal dialogue. When you study your reflection in the mirror, initially, you may notice your unconscious negative self-talk. When you engage in mirror work, you can hear and see it directly and redirect the narrative. You may notice thoughts like, "I hate my skin" or "Why are my eyes so big?" Instead of allowing them to beat you down, confront these thoughts and consciously reframe them. When you feel yourself focusing on something negative, it's your job to push the thought out of your mind and instead affirm your new identity—the identity that is in unconditional love with yourself. Use "I am" statements and powerful, uplifting affirmations that speak specifically to the physical attributes that bother or discourage you.

The most powerful form of mirror work comes from addressing your inner child. Speak boldly and say what you should have heard as an adolescent, the things that could have contributed to building your self-concept early on if they'd been said. Focus on statements like "Little (Your Name), I see you, love you, and I protect you" or "(Your Name), you don't have to prove your worth to anyone." At the beginning of this book, we discussed shadow work and how it's derived from things that traumatized you as a child and rewired your mindset, self-concept, and, ultimately, your life. The same shadow work will reveal your inner child's wounds. Use those wounds to cultivate specific empowering statements dedicated to the child in you. For me, I wasn't told enough that I was beautiful and powerful or worthy of being loved regardless of my shortcomings. I needed to know that just being me was enough to be loved. Little girl Mimi needed to understand that I didn't need to constantly perform and do magic tricks to gain attention or approval from those who loved me. Therefore, a good mirror statement I used frequently was, "Little Mimi, I know it may seem that your presence is insignificant, but understand your light shines bright no matter where you go or what you do. Even when you are silent, people still see and love you. It's not your job to worry about how others feel about your presence."

Take a moment now to reflect on what you would have loved to hear the most from your parents, siblings, and close friends. Write them down and recite them boldly in the mirror daily. Look yourself directly in the eyes and gaze into the mirror. Affirm and believe what you say wholeheartedly. Feel it deep within your soul. Practice speaking to your "future self." Ask her for guidance, support, and wisdom. You can recite phrases like, "Show me how to move in alignment with my highest self," or "I trust my powerful, magnetic nature," and "I am unapologetically entering my highest dimension." By affirming power, love, and abundance, you accelerate the process of 'becoming her.' These words don't just stay in your mind; they become imprinted in your subconscious, reprogramming your beliefs and self-concept. Your self-concept is rooted in the identity you claim for yourself. When you affirm, "I am here now," your subconscious believes it, and you begin to act like 'her' in your daily life. Remember, your subconscious doesn't know the difference between past, present, and future. Always state your desires as if they already exist so your mind can move in alignment to make them real.

Lastly, use your daily mirror gaze to cultivate a frequency of gratitude. Now, when you look in the mirror, instead of seeing your negative attributes right away, you'll begin to feel a high frequency of confidence. Become fully aligned and cultivate a heart filled with gratitude. Gratitude attracts abundance, joy, and love. When speaking to your future self, you activate the law of assumption: if you act as if something is true, it becomes true. Every time you look in the mirror and call in 'her,' you actually become her.

Sample Mirror Work Script for Building A Strong Self-Concept

- **Duration:** 10-15 mins per day
- **Location:** In front of a mirror (preferably a quiet, private space)

STEP 1: Grounding and Setting Intentions (1-2 minutes)

- **Breathe Deeply:** Take 3-5 deep breaths, inhaling through your nose for 4 counts, holding for 4 counts, and exhaling through your mouth for 6 counts.
- **Set Your Intention:** Speak this intention out loud:

  "Today, I choose to see myself through the eyes of love, power, and truth. I release all false beliefs and step into my highest self. I am ready to become the woman God created me to be, the woman of my dreams. Today, I choose to see my power clearly. I claim every part of me—my mind, my heart, my confidence, and my potential. I am here to rise."

STEP 2: Eye Contact and Self-Connection (1-2 minutes)

- **Look Directly Into Your Eyes:** Make direct eye contact with yourself in the mirror. Stare deeply into your own soul with intention. Avoid looking at other parts of your face or body.

- **Acknowledge Yourself:** Say your name (affirm your presence), and then add:

    "[Your Name], I see you. I honor you. I am proud of how far you've come. Thank you for showing up for yourself today and every day hereafter."

STEP 3: Self-Concept Affirmations (5-7 minutes)

While maintaining eye contact, repeat the following affirmations with energy and confidence. Feel every word. Activate the power within you and say them aloud with conviction.

- *"I am the main character in my life, and I vow to move as such."*
- *"I am the standard, and I rise to meet it every single day."*
- *"I am divinely made in God's image, and I reflect His power, wisdom, and love."*
- *"I am a woman of purpose, and I walk confidently in that purpose every day."*
- *"I am magnetic, bold, and unapologetic in my truth."*
- *"Today, I choose to love myself louder than any doubt or fear."*
- *"I release all shame and judgment. I am worthy of the grace, compassion, and kindness that I consistently extend to others."*
- *"I deserve peace, and I create it within myself daily."*
- *"I am beyond worthy of every opportunity, every dream, and every victory."*

- *"I am becoming the version of me I've always dreamed of, one decision at a time. I trust myself and God to lead me into my greatness."*

STEP 4: Gratitude for Self (1-2 minutes)

- **Place Your Hand on Your Heart:** Close your eyes for a moment and feel the warmth of your touch.
- **Acknowledge Your Growth:** Open your eyes, look directly into the mirror, and say:

   "I honor the version of me that never gave up. I honor the version of me that still shows up. I honor the version of me that I am becoming. Thank you for growing, learning, and evolving."

- **Name 3 things you're proud of:** Look at yourself with confidence and love and say:

   "[Your Name], I am proud of you for [name 3 things you are proud of yourself for, get deep, and of course, be intentional]."

   Ex. "I am proud of how I keep going, no matter how hard it gets."

STEP 5: Closing and Embodiment (1-2 minutes)

- **Visualize Your Highest Self:** Close your eyes and see your most powerful, confident, radiant self. See her standing tall, unshaken, unbothered, and unstoppable.

- **Step Into Her Energy:** As you open your eyes, see that version of you reflected back in the mirror. Say: *"She is me. I stand here already as everything I desire to be."*
- **Seal It With a Smile:** Smile at yourself with love and pride. Walk away feeling lighter, stronger, and more powerful. Vow to embody your future self in the remainder of your daily endeavors.

Do this mirror work every day for at least 21 days. If you want to amplify your experience, record yourself saying the affirmations and play them while you get ready in the morning. Your own voice amplifies the experience, sort of "tricking" your subconscious mind. Consistency is where the transformation happens.

Other Tips for Mirror Work

- Start Small: If 10 minutes feels too intense, start with 1-2 minutes.
- Don't judge your feelings: Feeling uncomfortable, emotional, or even teary-eyed is normal. Constantly tell yourself this is a part of the healing process.
- Speak with emotion: The more love and energy you put into your words, the deeper the transformation.
- Be Patient: Self-concept change doesn't happen overnight, but each session leaves an imprint.
- Make it a daily habit: Pair it with your morning or bedtime routine (Both if you need intense self-concept building).

Bonus Tip: Once you've started to regain the power within, start to incorporate your faith in God into your mirror work sessions. Add verses like:

"For God hath not given us the spirit of fear; but of power, and of love, and of a sound mind." -2 Timothy 1:7 (KJV)

"Fear thou not; for I am with thee: be not dismayed; for I am thy God: I will strengthen thee; yea, I will help thee; yea, I will uphold thee with the right hand of righteousness." -Isaiah 41:10 (KJV)

When life forced me into my deepest healing stage, I found myself in a lengthy period of isolation—not the isolation that builds you, but a self-inflicted isolation. My own former self-doubt transformed into a doubt I now feared in other people. I was no longer able to trust anyone fully. I believed that the people who didn't become fully submerged in and latch on to doing internal work the way I did surely wouldn't and couldn't understand this new and improved version of me. My gut and intuition told me to shine unapologetically in my radiance. Initially, it was hard; I really couldn't because I was afraid. I spent every waking moment protecting my energy and creating a sacred space within myself. I wanted to hide.

However, as I connected more deeply with God and my assignment began to be revealed, I kept getting messages that it was time for me to end my silence and my season of isolation. I was told I may be missing out on my destiny helpers or could in fact be someone else's destint helper. It was time to end the mystery of how I was able to ascend and instead embrace it and be more open to sharing about it. At first, my mindset was that there was no way I would feel safe here. I would not allow all the work I had done to be tainted by 'outside' connections.

See, the light was always there, even in the times when I thought it had dimmed. Others saw it; they always did. I'd just temporarily lost sight of it. My magnetic, radiant reflection had become a conversation starter. Women saw and craved that glow. Some embrace it, others reject it. Either way, they almost always acknowledged it. Little did they know, it hadn't come easy, and it was way more than just pretty privilege. It was destiny. Divine alignment. Testimony. Everything had happened just the way it was supposed to. I accept that now. Here I stand, exactly where I need to be, with a powerful toolkit like no other—life experience. You would never guess that I had once been strung out on ecstasy, homeless, rejected by my own family, a thief, and wandering the streets lost after the sudden and devastating death of Lamont.

In 2018, my cousin's suicide shifted my mind from being judgemental to being compassionate. I'd spent countless hours laughing with her, talking about the future, and reminiscing. I never knew she was hurting the way she was. For a long time, I blamed myself for being unaware of the real pain she felt. I had been so caught up in myself I didn't even notice the subtle signs. She constantly battled feelings of neglect, abandonment, and just never feeling worthy of being loved or like she was "enough." I, too, battled these same feelings. Despite our constant venting sessions about these stressors, I never in a million years would have thought she'd take her own life. Lamont held my hand through the entire ordeal. He gave me hope and empowered me to keep striving. He even tattooed her name. So, when I lost him, I snapped. I lost my power. I allowed chaos and desperation to become my new normal. I gave up on myself. I coped by living in an alternate reality of excessive drinking, drug use, and unhinged impulsive behavior. At one point, I thought I'd spend the rest of my life in depression, playing a game called life instead of actually living it. When you allow yourself to 'play the game,' you become addicted to instant gratification, external validation, and things that may feel good temporarily but not in the grand scheme of things. When you are actually living the life intended for you, you thrive. You feel happy, fulfilled, and aligned with your purpose.

The only thing special about me is I woke up. I became her. I became an alchemist. I chose to transmute everything that was sent to destroy me into power. That power became my story and led me right into my purpose. It couldn't have happened any other way. For years, I would refer to that phase in my life as wasted time, and the mere thought of it instantly sent a shot of regret through my nervous system. Now, I realize that my journey serves as living proof that transformation is possible—a complete one-hundred and eighty degrees.

Sidebar: You realize that for years, people have been saying three-hundred and sixty degrees, which actually means you'd end up right back where you started. But, in reality, the only things that you return to are the things you were called to do from the very beginning. The creative projects I was able to excel in as an adult were things I'd enjoyed doing as a kid. Reading, writing, expressing myself through my style, and being outspoken, to name a few. I'd ended up right back to little girl Mimi, who thrived in her creativity. They were all things I'd subtly been discouraged from pursuing early on. The more I was forced into more "realistic" or "normal" goals, the less time I had to actually explore my natural creative talents—my purpose.

When we begin to become our highest selves, our passion fuels us and keeps us inspired. High-frequency energy will flow naturally. When manifesting your destiny, your actions will be 'inspired' and not forced, like work or other unpreferred tasks. Your manifestation is brought to fruition through your passion. Your creativity pays you. Divine abundance. Freedom. Enlightenment. Growth, knowledge, and healing. Your journey to ascension serves as living proof that transformation is possible. When other women see you rise, they see what's possible for themselves. By embodying your radiant reflection, you become magnetic. You act as a mirror, reflecting their own potential back to them.

CHAPTER 9:

Your Infinite Reflection
Sharing your light with the world

∞

In growing my light, I fell in love with the effect it had on not only the people around me but strangers as well. More women wanted to know how I did it and what my "secret" was, especially those who knew about my troubled past. This became a pivotal moment in my transformation, a realization that assisted in my purpose being unveiled to me. Once you find your purpose, there's really no going back to the old you or your old life. It's like igniting the final fuel in creating the fire you need to walk boldly in your assignment. Your light equals someone else's breakthrough. Your courage to be seen and heard allows others to see what's possible for them. Understand that your story, your message, and your presence have the power to set other women free from the bondage of others' opinions. Free from the bondage of scarcity. Free from the bondage of their very own thoughts. Shine so bright that when they see you, they see God's goodness reflected back at them.

The reason why you feel you're meant for more is because you actually are. God planted purpose in your heart because you have one. Your purpose will always be tied to serving God's people in this natural world. The book of Galatians tells you about your requirement to live in alignment with the fruits of the spirit: love, joy, peace, longsuffering (patience), gentleness, goodness, faith, meekness (humility), and temperance (self-control). These fruits should be displayed externally as a direct result of the internal work you continuously commit to. The wisdom, talent, and ideas that God blessed you with aren't for you to hoard but are instead to be seen by the world. Someone out there is waiting on your book, your business, your testimony, or your words of encouragement. Stop looking for permission to be great. Your reflection is divine. Your light is necessary. Your story, your voice, and your self-concept are part of God's perfect plan for your life. It's finally time to stop being afraid to step fully into your greatness. Re-ignite and help others re-ignite. When you change the way you see yourself, you change the way you show up in the world. You don't have to be ready to be seen. You simply need to be willing. In order to be willing, you need to remind yourself of who you are. You must rebuild that undying love for yourself. You must rebuild your divine power. Don't you think you've dimmed your light for long enough? No more shrinking. No more hiding. The world is waiting for you to be seen, heard, and known. God is waiting for you to confidently embark on your assignment so He can release your divine blessings: the prosperity He promised you. Shine your light boldly, knowing that God is with you every step of the way. Your gut and your intuition are telling you to move forward in faith and power because that's your destiny. The world is waiting for you to show up as your authentic self. If you empower just one person to walk into their own light, you will be truly rewarded by God. Your self-concept is the root of everything. Changing your life and others' lives will require a divine and powerful sense of self. Your life can never rise higher than your identity. You cannot consistently outperform your self-concept.

> *"No man, when he hath lighted a candle, covereth it with a vessel, or putteth it under a bed; but setteth it on a candlestick, that they which enter in may see the light. For nothing is secret, that shall not be made manifest; neither any thing hid, that shall not be known and come abroad."-Luke 8:16-17 (KJV)*

The candle represents the light of God's truth and wisdom. Just as a candle is meant to provide light and visibility, so is God's word and light meant to be shared. You are called to live in a way that reflects God's light, allowing it to shine for others to see. You are unable to shine your light if you lack the confidence to do so. It is that simple. You have to relearn how to love yourself so that you can love others, and they, in turn, will love themselves.

Fill the world with the love from within, God's love.

"Let your light so shine before men, that they may see your good works, and glorify your father which is in heaven."- **Matthew 5:16 (KJV)**

Dear Me,

I come to you today to remind you that there's something extraordinary about you that the world has yet to fully experience. It's not your talents alone or even just your accomplishments; it's your spirit. It's the way you love, lead, and rise after every fall. That beautiful light within was placed there to be shared. I know that God didn't create me to blend in or remain unseen. My light is a testimony, a reflection of God's goodness in human form. Every challenge I've faced thus far has refined this light, only making it brighter and more unshakable. I understand that sharing my light doesn't mean that I have to be perfect. I am able and willing to be authentic and show the fruits of the spirit through me. I am committed to showing love that extends beyond convenience, joy that isn't dependent on circumstances, peace that quiets storms— both within and around me, patience that trusts in God's perfect timing, kindness that moves hearts, goodness that speaks louder than words, faithfulness that holds steady when everything around me shifts, gentleness that breaks cycles of anger and hate, and self-control that reminds me that discipline is a form of love. These fruits are the seeds I will plant in others with every interaction. I will constantly remind myself that my life is a ministry, even in moments when it feels ordinary. The world is waiting on my light, not a perfect version of me, but the real me. Every time I choose to shine, I give other women permission to do the same. I will rise, reflect, and radiate because I am worthy. Not for applause but for purpose. Not for perfection but for legacy. God has already qualified me and it's finally time for me to believe it and pay it forward.

With love,

ME

CHAPTER 10

Your Reflection

Your Revolution

∞

As you reach the final pages of this book, I want you to pause and acknowledge something truly powerful: You are a masterpiece in progress. Your journey toward self-love, growth, and transformation is not something that has a finish line. Your journey is a continuous process. Commit to empowering yourself. Commit to embracing self-love as a life-long journey. Commit to evolving and growing unapologetically. Without first cultivating faith in yourself, there's no way you can *genuinely* believe in things not seen that exist outside of you. The realization that I was required to co-create alongside God, using the powers He placed within me, truly changed my entire life. I stopped sitting around, waiting for somebody to come and save me. I put an end to self-sabotage. I started to speak life into myself daily. I ignored intentional, chaotic outside noise.

God blessed you at birth, but society subtly disempowered you. My assignment is to rebuild and rebirth. Your assignment now is to take heed and move forward in power. Consider me a reminder that there are people who still want to see you empowered wholeheartedly. Remember to use your words as tools, not traps. Love yourself undeniably and break down the societal mold that capitalizes on your perceived shortcomings. God makes no mistakes. You are exactly who you're supposed to be. Follow your heart and have faith in your intuition. Show up unapologetically. Believe in God's promises. More importantly, believe in the portions of him that live inside of you. Your power is supernatural. You are God-made and, therefore, God-body. You were created in His image; parts of Him were placed in you. Ask yourself daily, "What seeds am I planting with my time, energy, and decisions today?" "Are my thoughts contributing to my power or taking away from it?"

Be very mindful and very protective of your energy. Remind yourself that self-love is not about perfection; it's about grace, patience, and a willingness to meet yourself where you are with compassion. Understand that there will be days when you feel unstoppable and days when doubt will whisper obnoxiously in your ear. Be ready and willing to conquer both. You have overcome before, and you will overcome again. In order to meet your destiny, you will be tested to make sure you are ready to truly handle your assignment—the weight of the world. I transcended the moment I went from just living to understanding I had a purpose and assignment. I realized that there were a lot of women's lives in my hands. I became more empowered, knowing that truth and responsibility alone.

Each and every experience is a lesson, and every lesson is a step closer to your highest self, your dream reality. The most beautiful part of this journey is that you have the power to redefine yourself as often as you need to. You don't need permission or validation. Erase that from your mind today. Who you were yesterday does not limit who you can be tomorrow. With every sunrise, you have a new chance to show up for yourself with more love, understanding, and boldness than ever before. Growth is uncomfortable, but it is also constant. Elevation requires you to release parts of yourself that no longer serve you. But isn't that the beauty of it all?! You have the power to shed old versions of yourself like autumn leaves and make room for new, vibrant growth in the spring of your life.

I leave you with this encouragement: Promise never to stop evolving. Keep unlearning the lies you've been told about your worth, yourself, and your capability. Keep embracing the truth that you are fearfully and wonderfully made. Give yourself permission to dream audaciously, love yourself deeply, and rise boldly. You are worthy of every blessing you desire. Abundance is your birthright. Every step you take toward a higher sense of self-love is a step closer to the woman God created you to become. Your current challenges are not the end of your story; they're the beginning of a deeper, more profound relationship with yourself—a relationship that will ultimately save other women's lives. Hold your head high, keep walking forward, and know that with every challenge, you are becoming wiser, stronger, and more radiant. You are worthy. You are loved. You are capable. Most importantly, you are limitless!

Here is a letter from me to you in hopes that I've inspired you to love yourself wholeheartedly and unapologetically. It's time to walk in your divine power and abundance:

To every woman reading this,

I want to first give you your flowers for completing this book. Pause for a moment to acknowledge exactly what that means. You are committed to yourself—not just your growth, but to your God-like greatness. That kind of commitment deserves to be celebrated. It's not easy to face yourself, flaws, trauma, and all. It's not easy to challenge your old beliefs and rise into someone new. Still, you are dedicated to becoming her, and that's an achievement in itself. You are not ordinary. You never have been. There's something so powerful about a woman who understands her divinity. She moves differently, loves differently, and walks with a purpose that is undeniable. You are that woman!!! You are a vessel of God's love, strength, and grace. You are not a mistake. Every flaw you think you have is simply a reminder of your uniqueness. God doesn't make mistakes. He creates masterpieces! Confidence isn't about being the loudest in the room; it's about being anchored in the truth of who you are. You are not your mistakes. You are not your past. You are not the labels people tried to place on you. You are a reflection of God's glory, and when you walk in that truth, no one can convince you otherwise. Here are some very important things I'd like you to remember when the world attempts to dim your light:

- **Y*ou are worthy simply because you exist!***
  Reminder: You don't have to earn love, validation, or respect. It's already yours!

- ***You are powerful beyond measure.***
  Reminder: God didn't give you gifts, talents, and dreams just to watch them wither away. He blessed you with them to fulfill a purpose.

- ***You are enough!!!! Period. There are no qualifiers, no conditions, and no prerequisites.***
  Reminder: You are enough on your best day and on your worst day.

Stop shrinking. The world needs you to show up fully as yourself, not a watered-down, people-pleasing version, but the full, vibrant, unstoppable you. That's where your true confidence is found. Not in the applause of others but in the quiet knowing that you are exactly who God called you to be. Proverbs 31:25 (KJV) says, "Strength and honour are her clothing; and she shall rejoice in time to come." You wear strength as naturally as you wear clothes. You walk with honor even when nobody sees it. Rejoice because your time is coming. The seeds you've been planting will bear fruit. Walk boldly in your greatness. Speak with authority. Love without fear. Stand firm in your values. Be so grounded in your identity that no one can uproot you. You've done the work. Now, it's time to live it out. Don't just close this book and return to your old life and your old identity. Let this book be the beginning of something new. Let it be the spark that lights a fire in your heart. If you ever doubt yourself, come back to this letter. Remember who you are, whose you are, and why you were put on this Earth. You have a legacy to build, a life to live, and a light to shine. Don't dim it or doubt it. Allow yourself to walk in it fully and unapologetically.

With unconditional love, faith, and fire,

XO, MiMi

THIS ONE'S FOR YOU!!

I invite you to tap into your own creativity and curate a chapter of your very own. Name this chapter and speak about things that you found important in your own journey to embracing a new self-concept and cultivating lasting happiness.

Which part of this journey allowed you to feel most powerful? What message would you highlight the importance of for other women at the origin of their own journey of reclaiming their voice, confidence, power, and tapping into their divine destiny?

Share your enlightenment. Most importantly, share your own Dear Me letter that will re-ignite a spark in other women just like you!